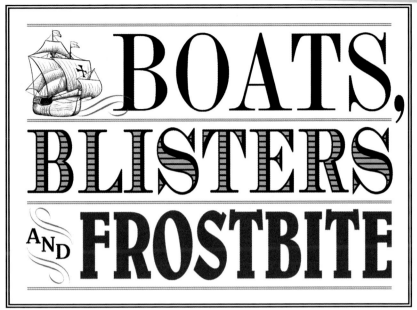

BOATS, BLISTERS AND FROSTBITE

METRO BOOKS
New York

An Imprint of Sterling Publishing Co., Inc.
1166 Avenue of the Americas
New York, NY 10036

METRO BOOKS and the distinctive Metro Books logo are
registered trademarks of Sterling Publishing Co., Inc.

© 2020 Quarto Publishing plc

ISBN 978-1-4351-7105-3

For information about custom editions, special sales, and premium and
corporate purchases, please contact Sterling Special Sales at 800-805-5489
or specialsales@sterlingpublishing.com

Manufactured in Singapore

2 4 6 8 10 9 7 5 3 1

sterlingpublishing.com

Design by JC Lanaway

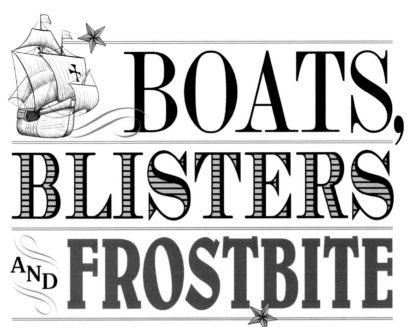

BOATS, BLISTERS AND FROSTBITE

The Story of Exploration Through the Ages

Jonathan J. Moore

METRO BOOKS
New York

CONTENTS

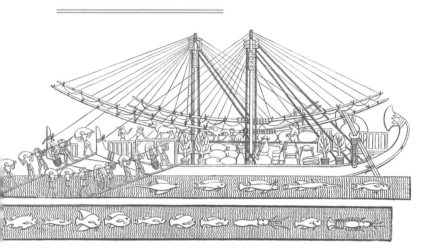

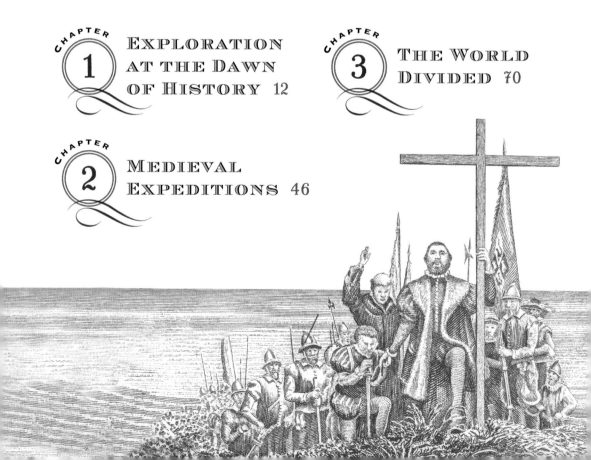

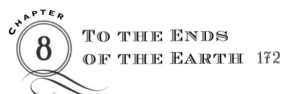

Introduction

THE URGE TO EXPLORE, to find new places, to move beyond the horizon and find fertile fields for hunting or farming is built into human DNA. Nothing demonstrates this better than the hominid settlement of Great Britain, which stretches

Neanderthal

back as far as 1 million years. Hominids include all of the great apes, including early humans and our ancestors. Britain's location between the Atlantic and continental Europe meant that the climate fluctuated wildly in this period and at least ten different waves of occupation have been detected.

The earliest inhabitants left tantalizing clues. A few primitive stone tools and some footprints were left by *Homo antecessor*, who wandered around between 1.2 million and 800,000 years ago. These tough ancestors of modern humans were surviving in temperatures similar to those currently found in Scandinavia. Subsequent extreme conditions may have left Britain uninhabitable until approximately 500,000 BCE when a new advanced hominid arrived. *Homo heidelbergensis* was a successful predator who left a plethora of stone tools used to hunt and butcher large animals such as horses, deer, and even rhinos.

The Anglian glaciation event set in approximately 450,000 years ago. Again, hominids were forced from the isles for many millennia. As soon as conditions moderated, another wave of explorers found their way to the lands recently released from the ice. These were our close relatives, the Neanderthals, who over the next several hundred thousand years would oscillate between their European homelands and Britain.

It appears that when Britain was cut off from Europe, between 180,000 and 60,000 years ago, it was again uninhabited. Then, around 60,000 years ago, Neanderthals made it back to Britain— crossing the great plains of Doggerland, a vast grassland that at one time joined Britain and Europe. Doggerland now lies beneath the North Sea, but fishermen trawling for shellfish sometimes haul up

LEFT **Woolly Mammoth bones were discovered in the North Sea in 2010 by trawlermen. These beasts roamed the icy tundra of Doggerland between Britain and mainland Europe until around 14,000 years ago.**

Norse longship

bones from extinct megafauna. Modern humans, *Homo sapiens*, finally reached Britain approximately 40,000 years ago, although even then their occupation was sporadic until permanent settlement was finally possible in approximately 12,000 BCE.

This picture of human exploration and expansion is radically different to the simplified picture of human occupation of the world painted by scientists as little as twenty years ago. It demonstrates that as soon as humans could move into a new territory, exploring its landscapes and utilizing its resources, they embarked upon the journey.

Up until approximately 50,000 BCE exploration had to be done by foot. A new technology was required to move beyond the Eurasian and African continents. The first step in this journey began when humans started to learn the art of seafaring. Indigenous Australian and Papuans crossed deep-water barriers to Sahul, the ancient continent by which Papua New Guinea and Australia were joined by a land bridge. They also penetrated into what is known as Melanesia and Micronesia, the large archipelagos off the shores of Papua.

Another technological breakthrough saw the ancestors of the people we now call the Pacific Islanders move from an ancestral homeland in the region of modern Taiwan and begin to penetrate the vast Pacific Ocean and settle the rich islands of Polynesia. This phase of exploration began in approximately 4000 BCE and finished with the Maori settlement of New Zealand a little less than 1,000 years ago.

In Europe, the first great seaborne explorers were the Minoan and Mycenaean Greeks who visited the eastern Mediterranean and explored as far as Italy and the Black Sea in the second millennium BCE. They were followed by the Phoenicians and the Classical Greeks who explored every aspect of the Mediterranean and even broke out into the Atlantic Ocean. Here further European exploration was stymied. The deep-bottomed trading vessels or the sleek-oared *biremes* of these peoples were not suitable for oceanic voyages.

It was only when the Scandinavian longships burst onto the scene that a European people was able to leave Eurasia and find a new continent. Sophisticated and seaworthy, these remarkable vessels enabled the Norse to penetrate deep into the Arctic Circle, as far east as the Caspian Sea and as far west as the continent of North America. Although impressive achievements, these explorations left no long-term change to the pattern of world settlement.

RIGHT The Maori used sophisticated longboats, rowed by twenty oarsmen, to establish the settlement of New Zealand.

Seven hundred years later, a handy little ship developed on the Iberian peninsula changed the future of exploration. The caravel and its larger cousins used a lateen sail that allowed them to sail to windward, or into the wind. All of a sudden, no sea or ocean was impassable. In the space of fifty years Africa was circumnavigated,

"HAD WE LIVED, I SHOULD HAVE HAD A TALE TO TELL OF THE
HARDIHOOD, ENDURANCE AND COURAGE OF MY COMPANIONS WHICH
WOULD HAVE STIRRED THE HEART OF EVERY ENGLISHMAN. THESE
ROUGH NOTES AND OUR DEAD BODIES MUST TELL THE TALE."

—THE DIARY OF CAPTAIN ROBERT FALCON SCOTT

African bird-eating tarantula

Australian kangaroo   African tapir

RIGHT Explorers not only had to put up with hostile temperatures and terrain, they also had to deal with novel and sometimes dangerous creatures.

much of North and South America were explored, and the first circumnavigation of the world took place. This furious burst of activity was mostly enacted by the brave and ruthless Portuguese and Spaniards. Exploration was invariably followed by exploitation and colonization. It appeared that these two Iberian powers could rule the world.

By the 1530s, other European naval powers were getting in on the act. England, France, and Holland sent canny explorers, funded by royal charter or trading companies, to find new lands and expand their own empires. Over the next three centuries, all of the world's oceans and seas were explored.

It appeared that the world was a European oyster. Only the hostile interiors of America, Australia, and Africa were left unknown and unconquered. The second great phase of overland exploration then followed, and in the nineteenth century the last mysteries of these hostile and exotic continents were finally solved.

Then only the poles remained. Once again new technology allowed intrepid explorers to reach the distant ends of the Earth, although not before many tragedies occurred in these frigid wastelands.

Just as the final explorers reached the poles, a new chapter of exploration was opened. When the Wright brothers conquered gravity in the first powered flight at the turn of the twentieth century, humanity looked upward for new fields to conquer. Sixty-six years after the first powered flight, humanity walked on the moon, in 1969.

LEFT Captain Scott poses next to a deep crack in the snow field, an example of how trecherous the ice could be.

RIGHT Buzz Aldrin salutes the American flag on the surface of the moon in 1969.

1

EXPLORATION AT THE DAWN OF HISTORY

As soon as hunter-gatherer societies settled into agriculturally based civilizations, the urge to explore the surrounding lands took hold. Even as early as 3500 BCE, Sumerian explorers set off down the rivers of the Fertile Crescent, traversed the Persian Gulf, crossed the Arabian Sea, and set up trading posts with the Harappan civilization in the Indus River valley. Some intrepid Sumerians may even have gotten as far as modern-day Sri Lanka.

LEFT The Sumerians developed a sophisticated culture that required a range of resources. They did not only rely on military force but also developed extensive trade networks.

EGYPTIAN EXPLORATION

The dynasties of Egypt sent many expeditions south to find the source of the Nile. Even this mighty empire could not solve the mystery of where the waters of this great river rose from the ground, and the source would not be discovered until the modern era. Nevertheless, the Egyptians did explore the Arabian Peninsula and discovered the Horn of Africa.

The first recorded voyage of discovery was sent out by the female Egyptian pharaoh Hatshepsut (reigned c. 1473–1458 BCE) to explore the fantastic land of Punt. Launched around the ninth year of her reign, the expedition was a triumph and they brought back trees that were successfully transplanted in Egypt—another historical first.

The cultures that followed—the Minoans, Greeks, Romans, Carthaginians, Vikings, and Imperial powers—launched themselves into the unknown. Some were searching for loot, some for trade, and some for glory. Whatever their motivations, the early explorers sent themselves into unexplored territory and faced innumerable dangers along the way.

ABOVE AND BELOW **Queen Hatshepsut sent several expeditions to the far reaches of the Nile River. Strange and wondrous objects were found in the land of Punt.**

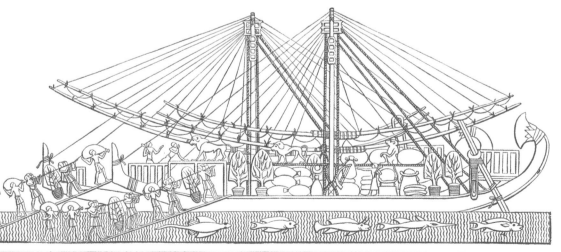

THE MINOANS AND MYCENAEANS

One of the first known seagoing empires was the Minoan empire based in Crete. It appears that peoples from ancient Asia Minor (Anatolia in modern-day Turkey) may have combined with Greek migrants from the Balkans to establish an empire that lasted for hundreds of years (c. 3000 BCE–c. 1100 BCE). From bases such as the palace of Knossos in Crete, these adventurers explored much of the eastern Mediterranean and set up trading stations throughout the Aegean Sea. Sometime during the fifteenth or fourteenth centuries BCE, their more warlike cousins from mainland Greece, the Mycenaeans, assumed control of Crete and supplanted the Minoans as the ruling class.

ABOVE **Marvelous frescoes discovered at the ancient city of Akrotiri give us a vivid portrait of Minoan seafarers. They dominated the eastern Mediterranean.**

The Mycenaeans, the heroes of Homer's *Iliad* and the *Odyssey*, were equally enterprising seafarers and there is evidence that they explored far beyond the bounds of their Minoan cousins. They investigated the coast of Asia Minor, setting up colonies there and even penetrating as far as Cyprus and Egypt.

Their most remarkable explorations were to the west. Traces of these explorers have been found throughout Italy, especially in Apulia (modern Puglia). Sicily probably housed several large settlements, and there is evidence of the Greek influence in Sardinia and even central Spain. It is likely that the Mycenaeans traveled through the Ionian Sea, the Adriatic, and the Tyrrhenian Sea. Some myths indicate that they may have even reached the Pillars of Hercules, the Greek name for the promontories that lie either side of where the Mediterranean meets the Atlantic Ocean.

Ancient Greek "myths" are not necessarily works of fiction. The word "myth" originates from the Greek word *mythos*, which can be interpreted as "true narrative," "word," or "tale." It appears that elaborate myths such as the tale of the *Theban Seven* and the *Sack of Troy by Agamemnon* might have been based on historical events. We have one Mycenaean myth that seems to tell a story of Greek explorers and the trials that they faced—that of Jason and the Argonauts, a tale that gives us a clear window into the past.

BELOW **The wealthy rulers of cities such as Mycenae sponsored ambitious voyages of discovery that penetrated into the western Mediterranean and east into the Black Sea.**

Jason and the Argonauts

The story of Jason and the Argonauts was, like most of the early Greek myths, a distillation of many events that took place over a long period of time. It deals with a hazardous expedition far beyond the bounds of Greek civilization into the treacherous and dangerous Pontos Axeinos—the modern-day Black Sea.

The tale tells of Jason, a dispossessed king, who returns from exile and is commissioned by the usurper of his throne to lead a group of adventurers to Colchis at the far reaches of the Pontos Axeinos. There they are to find the magical Golden Fleece and return with it as an offering. King Pelias, who sends Jason on this quest, is sure that he will perish and trouble him no more. This plan attests to the dangers of the journey; it would also indicate that many other Mycenaean Greeks had attempted the journey but failed.

Jason sets about preparing for the journey. As a noble he has the resources needed to conduct such an operation, another clear indication that merchant kings and warlords were at the heart of Mycenaean exploration. He commissioned the most talented boat-builder of his generation to build the *Argos*—a state-of-the-art ship around 70ft long, equipped with fifty oars and a sail. It was built of oak and pine and, with the goddess Athena's help, made sturdy enough to withstand the cruelest seas. The ship had a shallow draft that allowed it to navigate inshore waters without foundering. The rudder, anchor, sail, and oars could be removed—enabling the sailors to haul the *Argos* out of the water to avoid danger. The ship's figurehead had the power of speech and could offer guidance to the explorers. This is probably a reference to early navigational equipment. By orientating the figurehead north and the rudder south, the seafarers could align them with the stars above and get a fix on their location.

Once the *Argos* was built, it was up to Jason to select his crew. The myth tells of remarkable individuals being attracted from all over Greece. They had to prove their worth by competing in an athletic competition similar to the Olympic Games. Only the most skilled and healthy were allowed to join a perilous expedition into new and dangerous lands.

It was a very dangerous journey. The myth abounds in deadly creatures, seductive harpies, murderous women, terrible monsters, and hostile peoples. While these characters are likely to be metaphorical, the dangers they represent attest to the hostile environment in which the early explorers found themselves.

One key threat stands out in the tale of Jason and the Argonauts—the journey into the Black Sea was fraught with danger. First, the Greeks had

Fourth century BCE bronze coins depicting the galley *Argos*.

to pass from the Aegean through the narrow waist of water known as the Hellespont (today's Turkish Dardanelles). Strong winds and tides were natural dangers—as were threats from powerful states such as Troija (Troy) or pirates lurking ready to sweep down on any craft struggling against the rushing water. Once through the Hellespont, the Greeks entered the Propontis (Sea of Marmara), which took several days to traverse. Finally, they faced the greatest danger of all—the narrow Bosphorus Straight. Here treacherous, fast-moving currents tore through the confined waterway. In the Jason and the Argonauts myth, the rocky shores would clash together, smashing boats and killing any crewmen who braved the perilous waters. Only prayers to sea god Poseidon could save Jason and his men: The god is summoned to use his divine strength and hold the smashing rocks apart. Many crews must have been unable to row against the powerful currents and been destroyed when their boats were thrown against the rocky shores of the 20-mile waterway.

BELOW The *Argos* represented the cutting edge of Bronze Age technology. It allowed the Argonauts to negotiate difficult passages and discover new lands.

Once this perilous strait was negotiated the dangers were far from over. Bronze Age Greek boats were not built to withstand true oceanic conditions. They would hug the coast during the day, or make short trips between islands before sheltering in regular inlets and bays when night fell or if bad weather threatened. The Black Sea lacks many of these features. Its Greek name, Pontos Axeinos, means "the inhospitable sea." Wintry storms would whip up huge waves. Lacking inlets or islands, the early seafarers could find themselves exposed to the worst that the sea could throw at them. Cold winds from the east threw up conditions not found in the temperate Mediterranean—fogs, storms, snow, and even ice floes were regular hazards.

BELOW **The myth of the** *Symplegades* **(the clashing rocks) was a metaphor for the very real danger encountered by early sailors as they navigated the narrow Bosphorus.**

RIGHT The Golden Fleece was seized by Jason from the rulers of Colchis. By opening up a new trade route into the Black Sea, Jason ensured new riches flowed into Greece.

This lack of features also made navigation difficult. Should the Greeks try and find shelter on the bare shores, hostile locals such as the Scythians and Thracians might attack—and sacrifice their prisoners to bloodthirsty deities.

Jason and his crew finally got to their destination—the strange land of Colchis (modern Georgia) at the extreme eastern end of the Black Sea. Although they were welcomed, it was obvious that the strange customs and manners of the residents were intensely alien to the Greeks. The rulers practiced dark arts and were capable of evil magic that could summon monsters from the bowels of the Earth.

The fact that Jason was searching for a Golden Fleece is proof that the myth is based on knowledge of local customs. Even today in Georgia, a common method of searching for gold involves the use of sheep fleeces. The woolen hides are placed in mountain waterways where they trap gold particles suspended in the turbulent waters. This precious fleece motif also had echoes in the nearby Hittite empire. Located just south of Colchis on the shores of the Black Sea, this empire had a tradition of hanging sheep hides from sacred groves and temples as a symbol of royal power. Even the Etruscans in far-off Italy (who may have originated from Anatolia) understood a colored fleece to be a symbol of prosperity.

Amid much murder and mayhem, Jason escapes with the Golden Fleece and brings home as his bride Medea, the sorceress daughter of Aeëtes. She goes on to cause chaos and destruction, symbolic of the alien nature of the eastern barbarians.

While there is little evidence that the exploits of the early Mycenaeans led to permanent settlements in the Pontos Axeinos region, their trailblazing exploits eventually bore fruit. In the late eighth century BCE Greek colonies were founded all along the shores of the Black Sea. As well as taking the excess population from the Greek city-states, these colonies thrived on the export of timber, gold, slaves, grain, and other foodstuffs. Thanks to the efforts of Jason and his kind, the Pontos Axeinos became the Pontus Euxeinos—the welcoming sea.

The Ancient Greeks and Phoenicians

Around 1200 BCE, the Mycenaean empire collapsed. A combination of natural disasters and invasions from the north almost destroyed the old culture, and a dark age that lasted for 300 years descended on the Greek world. It is possible that Homer's poem the *Iliad* deals with conflicts from the period and that the tribulations suffered by the returning Greeks in his work the *Odyssey* are metaphors for the events of these troubled times.

BELOW The Phoenician cities on the coast of modern-day Lebanon established vast trade networks that stretched all the way from the eastern Mediterranean to the Pillars of Hercules.

But by 800 BCE, new Greek city-states began to arise out of the dark times of the past and these new societies proved to be more dynamic than even their Minoan and Mycenaean predecessors. The Greek *poleis* (city-states) were dynamic trading cultures that developed new boats to effectively navigate

the Mediterranean. For hundreds of years, adventurous expeditions would set out from Greece. They explored the western and eastern Mediterranean and established colonies wherever they could find vacant land and a good harbor. They even explored the Black Sea and established hundreds of viable colonies, including Massilia in France, Syracuse in Sicily, Taras at the heel of Italy, Byzantium on the entrance to the Bosphorus, Miletus on the south west corner of Turkey, and Cyrene in modern-day Libya.

ABOVE **Phoenician trading vessels had to be prepared to fight to protect their cargoes. If the fast *biremes* could not outrun attackers, mariners could put up a desperate fight.**

At this point, the eastern Mediterranean could almost have been known as the Greek Sea, while at the same time the western Mediterranean was controlled by the Phoenicians. Around 1000 BCE, the Phoenicians, explorers operating out of the towns of Tyre, Sidon, and Byblos in the Levant (all in modern-day Lebanon), sailed right across the Mediterranean and discovered the rich silver deposits of Spain. In the ninth century BCE Tyre founded Carthage in modern-day Tunisia and soon much of North Africa and Spain was conquered by these enterprising peoples. The Greeks and Phoenicians used their modern *biremes* (galleys with two rows of oarsmen) to dominate the great sea, and even now we are not sure what lands they discovered.

ABOVE **When Carthage was built on the shores of North Africa, a trading empire that held sway over the western Mediterranean and part of the Atlantic was established.**

Hanno and Himilco of Carthage

Carthage was destroyed by Rome in the Punic wars (264–146 BCE) and all its ancient records were lost. Thankfully, Greek and Roman writers retained some knowledge of Hanno and Himilco, Carthage's greatest explorers. Sadly, many of the details and dates of these journeys are rather hazy.

Hanno set off from Carthage sometime between 500–450 BCE to circumnavigate Africa. He was one of the first-known sailors from the Mediterranean to pass through the Pillars of Hercules and out into the Atlantic Ocean. *Biremes* were fast-moving ships that were perfect for fast travel in the more sheltered waters of the Mediterranean, but they were not appropriate for the high seas of the Atlantic. As such, it is likely that Hanno's expedition sailed in the round-bottomed *gauloi*. These merchant vessels could carry trade goods and supplies, and may have been reinforced with supports within the hull to help weather the fierce conditions found in the Atlantic Ocean.

A fleet of sixty ships was sent out in order to found colonies and gather information. Once on the north west coast of Africa, Hanno founded at least seven colonies in what is now Morocco. He continued southward along the coast of Africa trading with native populations: The Carthaginians were particularly keen on obtaining gold. Nobody is sure how far Hanno sailed. The ancient writer Arrian claims that he turned back after thirty-five days, while the Roman writer Pliny the Elder believed that the Carthaginian circumnavigated the entire continent and finished his journey with the discovery of Arabia.

Most modern scholars agree that Hanno probably got as far as modern-day Gabon in the Gulf of Guinea. This is supported by what appears to be an encounter with lowland gorillas. While exploring an island off the coast just before they turned for home, the expedition members came across a large population of hairy and savage people. Hanno ordered that some of these creatures, named *gorillai* by their interpreters, be captured. The larger males managed to escape, but three of the females were captured, killed, and skinned. The rough hairy hides were taken back to Carthage, where they could reportedly be seen hanging in a temple right up to the city's destruction.

ABOVE Hanno the Navigator was one of the first Mediterranean explorers to sail into the Atlantic Ocean. On his voyage of discovery, much of the African coast was explored.

Himilco's journey, taken around the same time as Hanno's, is equally shrouded in mystery. It seems, though, that he reached as far as Ireland. It is likely that the Carthaginian rulers organized this expedition to find new resources. In the early sixth century BCE they signed treaties with Rome and the Greek city-states. This meant that if the Carthaginians were to exploit new territories, exploration to the west was the only option. It has been suggested that Himilco was sent in the hope of finding new tin deposits. Tin, which constitutes just 0.001 percent of the Earth's crust, is an essential element in the production of bronze—a much-needed metal even in the Iron Age. Few locations had tin, but there were rumors that there were large tin mines located in the north.

Himilco first sailed along the coast of the Iberian Peninsula, possibly establishing some colonies near modern Lisbon. Proceeding to the coast of Gaul and the land of the Celts, the explorer came across a large promontory that has been identified as

Brittany. This region of France was known for its tin production—as was Cornwall in Britain, where it is likely that Himilco visited next. Several days' voyage followed and several ancient writers agree that he reached Iérnē, the Greek word for Ireland.

Himilco painted a dire portrait of the areas he visited, but this may have been a cunning ruse intended to scare the Greeks away from the newly discovered resources. He achieved his main aim and paved the way for Carthaginian traders who followed in his footsteps and established a direct trade route from Carthage to obtain tin.

It is even possible that the Carthaginian expedition got as far as the Baltic Sea. In the sixth century BCE, Greek writers told of a legendary river that flowed with amber. The river was called Eridanus—perhaps part of a tale told by one of Himilco's sailors? Three hundred years later these rumors proved to be true.

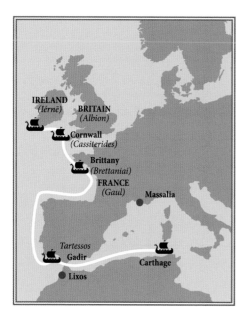

ABOVE AND RIGHT Himilco was sent by his Carthaginian masters to find new sources of the rare metal, tin. While some accounts have the explorer sailing around the Spanish coast (see map), some have him crossing through Gaul (modern-day France) before embarking on Celtic ships to continue his journey to Ireland.

Pytheas of Marseille

While Jason and his Argonauts may have been the first Greek explorers of the Hellespont and the Black Sea, almost 1,000 years later another intrepid explorer went to the "ends of the Earth." But Pytheas headed northwest not east.

Around 320 BCE, Pytheas of Massalia (now Marseille) in France sailed out of the Mediterranean, along the Atlantic coast, and all the way beyond the Arctic Circle. Massalia had been founded in 600 BCE by Phocaean Greeks who were considered the most adventurous of the Greek explorers. They were the first groups to venture far out beyond the Pillars of Hercules. Pytheas continued this tradition and upon his return, the Greek adventurer wrote an early travelogue titled *On the Oceans,* which was so filled with strange tales that many doubted the work's veracity.

The scientifically minded explorer estimated the latitude of his location by measuring the height of the sun at noon and the length of the days. As he ventured north, the days became extraordinarily long. From the tip of Scotland he sailed for six days before coming across the land called Thule. He noted that the sun was only below the horizon for one or two hours a day. Thule was inhabited by farmers who lived on millet, wheat, herbs, and honey. So wet was the land that they had to thresh their crops indoors or the constant rain would destroy them. The inhabitants enjoyed ale made from the grains, and mead made from honey. It appears that Thule is the first historical reference to Scandinavia.

It is estimated that Pytheas's landfall may have been at what is now called Trondheim Fjord in Norway—still one of this country's most fertile locations. The Greek then proceeded further until he came to the Frozen Sea.

He turned south and, passing modern-day Denmark, penetrated deep into the Baltic Sea. Here he solved an ancient mystery: Amber, called *electrum* by the Greeks, had been a valued commodity for thousands of years but no one knew where it came from. Pytheas found it washed up on shore, meaning that he was likely close to the Samland Peninsula near modern-day Kaliningrad. The Greek then probably traveled down the River Don to the Black Sea—predating the route the Vikings would take more than 1,000 years later.

ABOVE Pytheas is believed to be the first Greek to penetrate into the Arctic Circle. Warm clothes, not a traditional *chiton*, would have been required.

Xenophon

ABOVE Xenophon was a reluctant explorer. Stranded in the middle of the Persian Empire, he had to lead an army through hostile and strange lands.

Xenophon and the March of the Ten Thousand

The Greeks called the Mediterranean Sea their "pond." But while they had explored all of the coastlines, they rarely ventured more than a few miles inland. All of that changed with what became known as the Persian expedition, when Greek soldiers working as mercenaries marched into the heart of the Achaemenid empire—and almost got as far as fabled Babylon.

Approximately 11,000 Greek mercenaries had been assembled by the Persian prince Cyrus the Younger (died 401 BCE) in order to help him depose his brother, Emperor Artaxerxes II (reigned 404–358 BCE). They gathered in Sardis on the west coast of Anatolia and marched eastward through the mountains. For almost 1,500 miles they marched inland through the previously unexplored lands of Lycaonia, Cappadocia, and Syria, following the River Euphrates into the Persian Empire and through territory that no Greeks had seen before.

Finally, with Babylon lying just over the horizon, the two armies clashed at the small town of Cunaxa in September 401 BCE. Cyrus was killed almost immediately and his Persian army melted away to return home—leaving the Greek mercenaries stranded more than 1,000 miles from home.

The Persians managed to entrap and kill the Greek leaders and it was hoped that this would be enough to make the Greeks surrender, but it was not to be. A young Athenian called Xenophon (c. 431–354 BCE) rallied the troops and they set off to explore the Persian empire. The Greeks decided to head to the Greek colony of Trapezus on the Black Sea just to the west of ancient Colchis. This journey took two years and carried the Greeks through some of the most difficult territory in the Persian empire. Xenophon kept detailed records of the lands they explored and wrote them down in a fascinating travelogue—the *Anabasis*.

Their first major obstacle was in the mountainous lands of the Carduchians. These warlike people had once beaten an army of 120,000 Persians, who had disappeared in the mountains never to be seen again. By outflanking the roadblocks set up by the natives in steep mountain passes, Xenophon was able to march through the forbidding terrain.

The Greeks then traveled through the lands of Armenia and Cappadocia. In Cappadocia they found that all of the peoples lived in vast subterranean tunnels with huge storehouses for grain and their animals. The Greeks were well treated here and feasted on the abundant stores of food.

After fighting off the fierce warriors of Chalybes, who lived in hilltop fortresses, the Greeks finally saw the Black Sea and made their way to Trapezus and home.

ALEXANDER THE GREAT

Alexander the Great

Xenophon's expedition had demonstrated that the Persian army of the Achaemenid empire was vulnerable to the Greek heavy-infantry soldier. When Alexander's father, Philip of Macedon (382–336 BCE), equipped his infantry with 18ft pikes they became even more formidable.

Then Philip was assassinated. His son Alexander set out not only to fulfill Philip's dream of conquering parts of the Persian empire but also to conquer the world!

Alexander the Great and his army penetrated deep into western Asia. He was determined to keep going and wanted to reach the ends of the Earth. The Macedonian king was only finally halted by his mutinous army who thought that they had gone too far from their Greek homeland.

In 334 BCE the Macedonian army crossed the Hellespont into Asia. In a succession of battles, Alexander destroyed the Persian army and seized the heartland of the empire. Egypt, Anatolia, the Levant, and Persia all fell under Greek control.

After burning the Persian capital Persepolis, the army marched north to Media. Here Alexander and his Macedonian army saw the Caspian Sea and traversed the Caspian Gates.

BELOW In several years of campaigning, Alexander the Great united the east with the west and discovered many new lands and peoples who were brought into his empire.

The expedition penetrated into lands they had barely heard of: Hyrcania, Parthia, Bactria, and Sogdiana. The peoples of these mysterious lands—which roughly make up modern day Iran, Pakistan, Afghanistan, and central Asia—put up a furious resistance to the conquering Alexander. But none could stop him. Taking small groups of light troops, Alexander stormed hillfort after hillfort in what is now Afghanistan. Even today this country is notoriously hard to traverse, but Alexander managed this feat. The Macedonian king founded new towns as he progressed. Greek veterans were placed in the new settlements to consolidate his rule and all were named after the king. Kandahar in Afghanistan was originally named Alexandria.

The Macedonian army reached the limits of civilization at the Jaxartes River (the Syr Darya River in Kazakhstan). Here he defeated an army of nomadic Scythian horsemen. Not satisfied with these conquests, Alexander continued east until he came to the Himalayas and the Indus River. His exhausted army fought a series of battles against the Indian king Porus (reigned c. 326–c. 315 BCE). These battles were closely fought: The Macedonians faced heavily armored war elephants and four-horse chariots crewed by fierce warriors armed with 6ft bows. Even against these forces, Alexander and his all-conquering army were triumphant.

BELOW On the banks of the Indus River, Alexander discovered a civilization that rivaled the Macedonian Empire. King Porus used war elephants and heavy chariots.

After defeating Porus, Alexander planned to advance to the Ganges. But his army had had enough. In their view, they had passed the ends of the Earth thousands of miles back. Alexander was reluctantly forced to turn for home. But he continued to explore new lands. The army turned south and returned to Babylon after exploring southern Iran, Iraq, and some of the Arabian Peninsula.

When Alexander returned to Babylon, he set in motion new plans of exploration. He wanted to circumnavigate the Arabian Peninsula and there were even rumors that the king wanted to turn west and conquer Italy. These plans never came to fruition, however, because Alexander died in 323 BCE.

BELOW Alexander's thirst for exploration and conquest would have seen him find many new lands had he not been struck down by a mysterious illness after entering Babylon.

The Macedonian's amazing record of exploration and conquest opened up routes through which trade and knowledge continues to flow even today.

Admiral Nearchus

Alexander tested the limits of the Greek world, but he was not on his own. One of his most loyal and trusted subordinates was Admiral Nearchus (c. 360–c. 300 BCE).

Fortunately for Alexander, he had the talented Nearchus under his command. When the Macedonians reached the Indus River it was noted that crocodiles very similar to those found in the Nile lived in its waters. Alexander thought that the Indus may have been the source of the Nile and that India and Africa could be linked. To test the hypothesis, he had Nearchus build a fleet of galleys. The fleet of 150 ships loaded up a quarter of Alexander's more footsore soldiers and navigated down the Indus River during 326–325 BCE until it reached the Indian Ocean. It was no easy passage and many of the local inhabitants sought to stop the fleet.

From there, the fleet turned west and followed the coast until it came to the straits of Hormuz, the entrance to the Persian Gulf. The admiral was a gifted cartographer and kept an accurate record of the harbors and natural features he encountered. After navigating the Gulf, the fleet rejoined the army before it proceeded to the mouth of the Tigris.

Many strange and wonderful things were described in the admiral's journal. He described one tribe who lived on the coast. He called them the "turtle eaters" since their diet largely consisted of turtles and they used their shells to roof their houses. This remarkable people were covered in dark shaggy hair and wore clothes made out of fish skins.

As well as bringing many tall tales to the Greek world, Nearchus had opened a new route between the East and West, allowing new products and ideas to flow into Europe.

ABOVE **Alexander's admiral Nearchus navigated all the way from the headwaters of the Indus River and into the waters of the Persian Gulf.**

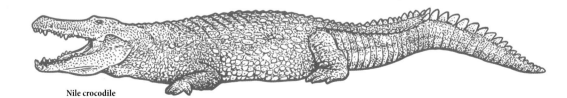

Nile crocodile

Legionaries at the Edges

Some units of Roman soldiers explored the outer reaches of civilization against their will, with some ancient writers describing Roman legionaries as far afield as China and Ireland.

At the Battle of Carrhae against the Parthian empire in Mesopotamia in 53 BCE, a Roman army of seven legions (50,000 men) under Crassus (c. 115–53 BCE) was decimated. Only 10,000 men survived, but they were captured. It appears that they were marched to the eastern border of the Parthian empire, where they were posted as border guards against enemies such as the Han Chinese.

Approximately twenty years later, a strange group of foreign fighters who arranged their shields like "fish scales" (possibly a reference to the Roman army's *testudo* defensive shield formation) popped up on the border of the Han empire and Tibet in a garrison town called Li-Jien. Legionaries maybe? Perhaps they were captured by the Han from the Parthians or were hired as mercenaries. Even now many of the inhabitants of modern-day Li-Jien have Caucasian DNA, indicating they could be descended from these Italian-born soldiers.

ABOVE **Romans did not win every battle. It is possible that some of Crassus's soldiers were defeated by the Parthians and ended up in China!**

A similar tale appears about Ireland. After 83 CE, the Romans withdrew from the northern regions of the British Isles, but there is some evidence that Nero's general, Agricola, sent a small military mission to explore the coastline of Ireland. They may have been captured, and Irish legends tell of a mighty warrior that had ten arms and ten legs and fought covered in scaly hide—once again, a possible reference to a Roman *testudo* formation.

VIKINGS CONQUER THE WORLD—ALMOST

When Vikings struck at Lindisfarne in 793 CE, it seemed to Europeans that a terrible new threat had emerged from out of the blue. In fact, Viking explorers had been building their knowledge of the seas surrounding Scandinavia for nigh on almost 1,000 years. Utilizing the remarkable technology of their longboats and developing navigation skills that were second to none, the Norsemen (Northmen) from modern-day Norway, Denmark, and Sweden explored the coasts of northern Europe, the Mediterranean, and even the Black Sea. Perhaps the most remarkable accomplishment was the Viking discovery of Greenland and North America. If it were not for an accident of history, the fierce Norseman might have colonized the entire continent.

Viking longboat

BELOW **The Vikings learned to read the sea and landscape when navigating. Huge fog banks or periods of long calm were a real danger.**

The Beginnings of Norse Exploration

Even as Pytheas was visiting Thule in the fourth century BCE, the inhabitants of that remote region were laying the foundations for their own extraordinary feats of exploration. A remarkable discovery on the Danish isle of Als reveals that the Iron Age inhabitants were already developing the technology that would allow them to build their famed longships. In a bog at Hjortspring, a long war canoe was discovered. It was nearly 60ft long and 6ft wide, with distinctive double-beaked prows at either end, just like the later longships built by Viking descendants. Most remarkable was the method of building this large vessel. It was built from long limewood planks with a broad bottom piece and other overlapping planks on each side. These boats are known as clinker-built boats and the planks were sewn together and fastened with ropes while the entire structure was strengthened with internal ribs. This building method produced a shallow-keeled vessel that was perfect for raiding in internal waterways but had a strength and flexibility that allowed it to brave even heavy seas. The boat had a steering oar at either end, allowing it to face in either direction. It was propelled by crews equipped with paddles—suitable for shorter voyages, but without a sail these earlier boats were not built for oceanic trips.

BELOW **The remarkably flexible design of the Viking longboats allowed them to weather the highest seas and navigate shallow inland waterways.**

In the third century CE, Norse boat-building had not yet developed ships capable of long sea voyages, with vessels called *als* being paddled by up to twenty crewmen. While this method of propulsion can produce short bursts of speed suitable for a war canoe, it is not suitable for long voyages, as the crews would soon become exhausted. Boats discovered in southern Jutland at Nydam

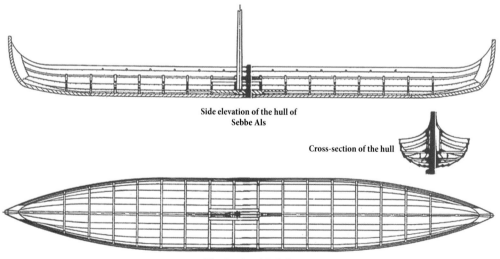

Side elevation of the hull of
Sebbe Als

Cross-section of the hull

Plan drawing of the hull

Moss in 1863 had the characteristic clinker-built hulls and the long raking prows. However, they were strengthened with iron nails and had ports to allow them to be rowed using long energy-efficient oars. What's more, the sole rudder was firmly attached to the side of the ship on a wooden boss, allowing for sustained and accurate navigation of the vessel. It is estimated that these boats were built right at the end of the third century CE.

Only one more modification was needed before these agile boats became truly useful for long seaborne voyages—the invention of a sail. It is not known exactly when the Scandinavians adopted this technology, although the Celts and Germans used the sail in their boats well before the Roman invasion in the first century BCE. It seems likely that the Norse began to use the sail when they first left their fjords and lakes in the sixth and seventh centuries CE. Two types of boats were crucial to Norse exploration. The sleek shallow-hulled longboat was used for raiding and warfare, while the *knarr* were deeper, broader, and sturdier—ideal for carrying cargo and even livestock. These trading vessels depended on wind power for long journeys, but could resort to oars for finer maneuvers.

One thousand years of development enabled the Norse to create seaworthy ships unsurpassed in history for centuries. Abundant timber allowed them to craft different types of boats so that they were as comfortable on open water as in coastal waters. The continual use of deeper-bottomed trade ships, fishing vessels, ferries, and even simple rowing boats meant that Norsemen developed an intimate understanding of the ocean and its ways.

The longboats and *knarr* had a central spine carved from a single trunk, with the clinker-built hull rising from the sides. The oak or ash planks were finely trimmed and then waterproofed with horse hair or wool soaked in boiled tree sap. Ribs and crossbeams strengthened the hulls and these were covered with a deck and benches made from pine. The huge square sails were made from pieces of woolen or linen fabric, which were stitched together and covered in animal fat to make them waterproof and to ensure that every breath of wind was captured. The main mast could be lowered when approaching a hostile shore or in rough seas.

Norse society was uniquely placed to exploit this technology. Warm Atlantic Ocean currents made agriculture viable in Scandinavian lands, and this combined with rich fisheries led to strong population growth. Arable land was finite, leading to a large surplus population looking for new land to settle.

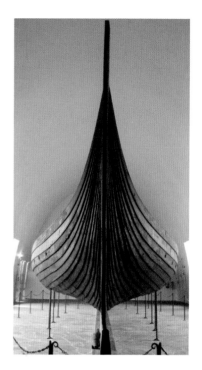

ABOVE **The single central spar of the longboats, seen here in a boat at the Viking Ship Museum, Oslo, lent great strength to the ships.**

Scandinavian society had always been violent, with different settlements raiding their neighbors on a regular basis. Interaction with the Romans led to an increasingly formalized militarization of society, in which warlords and kings would attract a following of warriors who swore to use their swords in the service of their lord. This was conditional upon the leader furnishing them with food, lodgings, booty and, most importantly, victory in battle. By the sixth and seventh century CE many Scandinavian tribes had coalesced into centralized states. But these were still unstable. Many Norse warriors had enough prestige to claim kingship as any man possessed of royal blood through the maternal or paternal lines could claim a throne. If they could not take on one of the larger states or were defeated and sent into exile, they could become a "sea king"—a king who lacked land but commanded the loyalty of a crew of hardened warriors. These sea kings could engage in pirate raids or seek to find land elsewhere. Even established rulers of the new states would go raiding to reward their *huscarls* [servants] and *jarls* [chiefs] while adding to their prestige.

At the most basic level, an individual leader who could afford (or build) a boat could crew it with landless volunteers and set off on a journey of exploration and adventure.

Sagas written at the time echo the remarkable achievements of the Viking explorers. Placenames within these tales attest to their journeys—Wales is named Bretland, Novgorod in Russia is Holmgard, Cyprus is Kipr, Gibraltar is Nørvasund, and the golden city of Constantinople (modern Istanbul) was called Miklagard— perhaps an echo of Valhalla, the Viking home of the gods, with its 640 doors and a reflection of the massive towering walls that guarded the ancient imperial capital.

Scandinavians had a long tradition of exploration and migration. The first recorded historical event was the Cimbrian War of 113–101 BCE. The Teutones and the Cimbri migrated from the Jutland Peninsula—modern-day Denmark— and cut a bloody swathe through Gaul (France) and down the Italian Peninsula. They destroyed several Roman armies on the way, but were all but wiped out in the final battle against the Roman general, Marius (c. 157–86 BCE).

During the collapse of the Roman empire, several Germanic tribes who claimed descent from Scandinavian tribes made up part of the barbarian hordes who took over part of the former empire's western territories. The Angles, Saxons, and Jutes settled in Britain, while the Heruls attacked France and penetrated down to the Ukraine into the Black Sea and even as far as the Mediterranean.

By the seventh and eighth centuries CE, a new wave of Scandinavian explorers combined trade and conquest throughout much of the known world. They penetrated down the Russian river systems to the Black Sea. Here the flexibility of the longboats gave them the edge in the shallows of the mighty rivers such as the Don and the Volga. Where river systems almost intersected, the explorers could hoist their boats out of one river and travel overland on logs to the adjacent system—opening up new territories and allowing them to penetrate as far as the Caspian Sea and beyond. Scandinavian colonies were founded in Poland, Finland, and the Baltic states as bases of exploration. Based on the cities of Novgorod and Kiev, the Scandinavians, or Rus as they were known to the locals, dominated the local Slavic populations and established a large empire covering much of what we now know as Russia. By 923 this extended from the Gulf of Finland down to the Crimea on the Black Sea.

In 793, true seafaring became part of the Viking repertoire and their navigators guided the fast-moving longships onto Lindisfarne on the coast of the British Isles. By 830, Vikings reached the Black and Caspian seas and traded with Constantinople and even Baghdad, showing that they made their way down the Tigris and Euphrates. Some Indian ceramics and jewelry has been found in the Norse homeland, so it is even possible they penetrated as far as the subcontinent. In 844, Viking explorers attacked the Islamic states on the Iberian Peninsula. The al-Urdumaniyin (Arabic for "Northmen") struck terror on the Atlantic and Mediterranean coasts.

BELOW **The dragon heads of Viking longboats were a symbol of terror throughout the known world as the Norse explored the Mediterranean and as far as the Caspian Sea.**

Viking Navigation

How did Norsemen perform such spectacular feats of navigation and exploration in some of the most difficult environments on Earth? On the journey to Greenland from Europe, Norse seafarers had to cross more than 2,000 miles of treacherous ocean waters. In the ninth century only the Malays in the Indian Ocean or Polynesian settlers in the Southern Pacific Ocean were capable of performing similar feats — although they did it in a much kinder environment.

Each ship or fleet had a specialist to help them traverse these difficult seas. Viking navigation was carried out by a pilot. These professional seamen called upon generations of sea lore. They did, of course, also refer to celestial bodies such as stars, but in the Arctic region bad weather often hid these navigational clues.

Vikings had an impressively intimate understanding of the sea and were able to use all five senses to detect the moods of the ocean and use their intuition to estimate their location. They learned the routes used by animals such as whales or herrings on their annual migrations. Familiar landmarks were fed into their mental maps. Mariners kept an alert ear out for the sound of breakers in the distance or the cry of seabirds. They could smell land on a sea breeze and

ABOVE The most important man on a Viking ship was the navigator. He drew on knowledge accumulated over many generations to complete a successful voyage.

taste changes between saltwater and glacial runoffs. Viking poems, chants, and songs detailed sea routes, while navigational hazards were handed down through the generations.

Pilots also used latitude sailing, where they would sail along the coast until they were at the same latitude as their destination, and when there was a favorable wind set off heading due east or west until landfall was made. The location of the sun during daylight hours or the North Star at night allowed the pilot to ascertain their latitude, but there was no similar aid to determine longitude. They had to rely on dead reckoning or try and estimate the speed at which they were traveling—not a precise science.

Birds were also a valuable aid to navigation. Ravens were often carried onboard longboats. A released bird would fly off toward land to be followed by the fleet. Should the bird return, there was little likelihood that landfall was in the offing.

On his journey to Iceland in the ninth century CE, Floki Vilgerdarson took three birds on his journey to Iceland. The first raven that he released flew back in the direction of the land they had left; the second circled the fleet before returning to its basket; but the third flew straight ahead. Floki followed the raven and soon his fleet made landfall.

Most sailors track the location of the sun to get an idea of their latitude. Vikings may have used several ingenious devices to detect the location of the sun in the thickest of overcast conditions. A circle of wood with an upright gnomen (the upright section of a sundial) was floated in a bucket to keep it steady and immune from the swell of the ocean; even the vaguest of shadows could reveal the location of the sun.

Another possibility is that the Vikings used sunstones in conjunction with sundials. These crystals could be carved to refract and concentrate the sun's rays even on cloudy days. This clear, glasslike rock can be passed across a mariner's visual field to reveal the location of the sun. The wreck of an Elizabethan man-of-war that sank near Alderney in the Channel Islands in 1592 yielded fragments of sunstone near other navigational aids—indicating that it could have been part of a mariner's navigational kit for many centuries.

LEFT **One of the most important tools for a Viking explorer was a raven. These birds could detect land many miles away.**

Closing the Circle—Vikings in the North Atlantic

Many thousands of years earlier, Asiatics had moved east across the Bering Strait to colonize America. Around the year 1000 Leif Erikson (c. 970-c. 1020) sailed west from Greenland and contacted the descendants of these early Americans. For the first time in history, humans had visited all parts of the globe.

The journey to Vinland, as Erikson named the continent of North America, was a long time in the making. The Norse were familiar with the Orkneys at the northern tip of the British Isles, and from there it was a short trip to the Shetland islands and the Faroe archipelago. A further 450-odd miles to the northwest found Iceland and a similar voyage landed them on the southern tip of Greenland. In a westward direction was Vinland.

It seems that Irish monks discovered some of these lands centuries before the Vikings. Irish monks loved solitude and knew where best to find it on windswept islands in the North Atlantic. They set out in hide boats called *currachs* and established religious settlements. The monks certainly reached the Faroe Islands. When the Norse settled there in the early ninth century they found the fertile islands inhabited by large flocks of sheep—no doubt brought there by the Irish monks for sustenance and warmth.

The next step was Iceland. This was discovered almost by accident. Around 860 CE, Gardar the Swede set out from Denmark toward the Orkneys. A mighty storm arose and his ship was swept far out into the Atlantic. After days and weeks adrift, Gardar saw a

BELOW **The Vikings who discovered Iceland were able to eke out a precarious existence on the windswept land.**

forbidding land on the far horizon. This was the dangerous cliff-filled south coast of Iceland. The brave explorer followed the coastline until he had circumnavigated the land and proved that it was an island. Gardar spent a year exploring the island, which he named Gardarsholm, before returning to Norway.

Other adventurers followed. One Norwegian called it Snowland and Floki Vilgerdarson called it Iceland—the name that stuck. Soon a steady stream of settlers arrived in the new land and by 900 there may have been 20,000 people there, hailing from all over Scandinavia. A dialect remarkably similar to the original language of these Scandinavian explorers is still spoken in Iceland. Since settlers from disparate populations had to get along, they still spoke the commonly used Old Norse—the lingua franca of the day.

In 975–976, there was a poor crop in Iceland and Erik Thorvaldsen (c. 950–c. 1003), later known as Erik the Red, was forced to leave Iceland for three years to avoid a blood feud. He decided to head for Gunnbjorn's Skerries and see if he could settle there. Erik's expedition made landfall near a glacier on the east coast of the new land. He decided to explore further and followed the coast south, rounding Cape Farewell, the island's southernmost tip. His determination paid off when his expedition came across the sheltered western fjords. The lands here provided good grazing and abundant timber.

The Icelanders had arrived at a period when there was a window of good weather appropriate for farming. Between 900 and 1250 CE, the climate of the Northern Atlantic was subject to what scholars

BELOW **When Eric the Red brought settlers to Greenland, they must have wondered why the harsh glacial island had such a pleasant name.**

call the Medieval Warm Period. When this altered and the climate became colder, the last Scandinavians were forced to leave Greenland and abandon their farms.

But this was in the distant future. Erik returned to Iceland after his three years of exile and, dubbing the new land "Greenland," sought to attract new settlers. Two settlements were founded and one of the new inhabitants was Erik's son Leif.

Leif was like his father—a keen adventurer. Leif used the sighting of a fellow Viking blown off course to inspire him to discover a new land. In 986, a merchant from Iceland was sailing to visit his father in Greenland. Bjarni Herjolfsson was blown off course and lost in fog for many days. He came upon a densely forested, hilly land. However, he decided not to investigate further but instead turned the prow of his ship eastward and four days later came upon his original destination.

BELOW Leif Erikson's expedition sights the continent of North America—the entire globe had now been circumnavigated by humans.

Bjarni was called lots of unfavorable names for refusing to land on the new territory, despite the entreaties of his crew. Leif purchased Bjarni's boat and set out to find the new territory. He asked Erik if he wanted to accompany him on the voyage of exploration but his father considered himself too old.

Leif sailed northwest and came upon a land of bare rock and glaciers. He named it Helluland ("Slab Land") and it is likely that this location is modern-day Baffin Island. It is a remarkable thought to consider that by landing at Helluland he was closing the circle of human exploration of the globe—being the first recorded European to set foot on the American continent.

Erikson went ashore, going one better than the timid merchant Bjarni. Traveling south, the expedition reached Markland ("Forest Land"), most likely Labrador. Going further south, he reached a fertile land where the rivers were filled with salmon and wild grapes grew in profusion. Leif called this region Vinland ("Wine Land") and this was probably somewhere in what is now known as New England.

His brother Thorvald was known for a heinous act. During his expedition in 1003, upon landing in Vinland, he came across three humps on a beach. These proved to be upturned canoes with nine indigenous men sheltering under them. Thorvald promptly ordered that the people he called *skraelings* ("foreigners") be killed. Eight were butchered but one fled and returned with reinforcements. Thorvald received a mortal wound in his armpit. He had the dubious distinction of being the first European to massacre Native Americans and the first to die at their hands! The indigenous men he killed were probably Thule, ancestors of the modern Inuit.

Leaving America

One of the perennial mysteries of history is why the Norse did not settle permanently in North America. The remains of several Norse settlements have been found, including one in what is now known as L'Anse aux Meadows, a site on the northern tip of Newfoundland, Canada.

Two Icelandic sagas, *Erik the Red's Saga* and the *Saga of the Greenlanders* describe these early settlements and both describe the *skraelings*, the name the Norse gave to any peoples who did not have Scandinavian origins, just as the Greeks described foreigners as barbarians. The origin of the word is obscure but could have at its root the old Norse terms *skra*, which means "skin," and could possibly refer to the animal skins that the indigenous inhabitants wore instead of wool. It appears likely that the Norse came into contact with two indigenous groups: the ancestors of the Inuit to the north, and perhaps the Iroquois to the south. Initially relations were peaceful and the settlers traded metals for furs while harvesting timber and even making wine. For some reason relations between the groups deteriorated and they were soon in open warfare.

Whatever the truth behind the reasons for leaving Vinland, the Vikings packed up all their goods, took their livestock and ploughs, and left for Greenland without even leaving graves to mark their passing.

Maybe the small colony on Greenland, thousands of miles from North America, did not have the resources to establish a settlement in a land already occupied by a large number of indigenous inhabitants.

RIGHT There is only one confirmed Norse settlement in North America, depicted here at L'Anse aux Meadows. There may have been many more.

AHMAD IBN FADLAN

THE YEARS BETWEEN 800 and 1300 CE can be considered the Golden Age of Islam. During this period engineering, medicine, art, science, and literature flourished. So, too, did exploration.

One of the best-known of the earlier Arab explorers was Ahmad Ibn Fadlan (877–960 CE). He explored deep into the heart of modern-day Russia and reported on the remarkable customs of its peoples.

In 921, he left Baghdad as part of a mission to teach Islamic law to the Bulgars, who had recently converted to Islam. These ancestors of modern Bulgarians were residing on the banks of the Volga River. First the Arabs had to travel through Persia before going through the central Asian cities of Samarkand and Khiva. They then proceeded up to the Caspian Sea and encountered fierce tribes such as the Pecheneg and Bashkir. After a year of exploration Ahmad finally came upon the Bulgars in their capital Bolghar.

Ibn Fadlan spent at least a year teaching these people. While there, he and his companions noticed that womenfolk were held in high regard. They could sit and eat as equals with the men and even bathed nude in public.

 **One of the first ever travelogues was written by Ahmad Ibn Fadlan. He included many salacious details when writing about the Norse.**

While in northern Europe the Vikings were mainly engaged in rape and plunder, in the south they were chiefly involved in trade. He noted that the Norse were a well-built and handsome people as tall as "palm trees" and covered in tattoos.

Ibn Fadlan's reports on the pagans that he encountered on his travels are very useful to historians. Soon many of the peoples he encountered, including the Rus, would convert to Christianity—ushering in the Middle Ages.

CHAPTER 2

MEDIEVAL EXPEDITIONS

THE HISTORY OF EXPLORATION IN THE MIDDLE AGES is dominated by three figures: Marco Polo from Christian Europe, Ibn Battuta from the Muslim Arab lands, and Zheng He of the Chinese Ming empire.

All three explorers dedicated much of their life to finding new lands. Marco Polo and Ibn Battuta relied on the Silk Road for much of their travel, while Zheng He navigated new lands in a huge fleet of Chinese junks fitted out especially for exploration.

Yet by the end of the medieval period, two whole continents remained to be fully discovered by European and Eastern explorers—America and Australia. Or did they?

LEFT Henry the Navigator (left) and Marco Polo were pioneers in the field of exploration. While Polo wrote an imaginative travelogue, Henry sponsored new scientific methods.

MARCO POLO AND THE SILK ROAD

When Venetian merchant brothers Niccolò (c. 1230–c. 1294) and Maffeo (c. 1230–1309) Polo set off to the empire of Kublai Khan (1215–94) in c. 1260, and later with Niccolò's son Marco (c. 1254–1324 BCE) in 1271, they were embarking on a journey along a route—the Silk Road—which had been in operation for almost 1,500 years.

The route that stretched from the heart of the Chinese empire all the way across the Eurasian continent to the Mediterranean Sea came about as part of a plan to open the empire up and create new trade links, instigated by Emperor Wudi (156–87 BCE) of the Han Dynasty. Wudi sought to purchase horses from the Steppe nomads and precious objects from what is now India and Pakistan, expanding (and taxing) on the limited trade that was already established between East and West.

Wudi sent out a diplomat named Zhang Qian (died 114 BCE) to try and find a route westward and set up trading contact with the nomadic horsemen of the Steppe. Over two expeditions, Zhang Qian explored the regions bordering the Han Empire, and by taking goods along to trade he established alliances with the fierce Yue-Chi nomads. Thus the Silk Road was born.

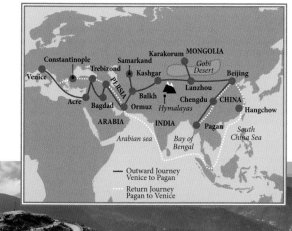

LEFT AND BELOW Marco Polo traversed vast tracts of land and sea. Traveling on the Silk Route between China and India posed many challenges.

Setting out from the eastern edge of the Himalayas, the route went south of the Gobi Desert, through Gansu, and skirted the Taklamakan Desert. A huge organized workforce of men was employed building roads, setting up way stations, and fortifying towns. The route went through Kashgar and this became a vast entrepôt, where the produce from the subcontinent and China crossed over. From here the route continued to Samarkand and Merv, before it skirted the southern shores of the Caspian Sea and then proceeded through Persia to the Mediterranean. Both Samarkand and Merv became powerful city-states at the "crossroads of cultures."

Precious goods flowed between Europe and India to China, including, obviously, silk, as well as jewels, and spices, and even early gunpowder found its way from China to the West. When the Mongol empire arose in the early thirteenth century, the eastern route of the Silk Road moved north so that it passed through Karakorum, the capital founded by Ghenghis Khan (1162–1227), and security along the entire route was strengthened through the use of regular way stations. By the time Monkge Khan (1209–59) (Ghenghis Khan's grandson) ascended the Mongol throne in 1251, it was claimed that a person with a pot of gold balanced on their head could walk across the entire empire without fear of robbery!

BELOW **The Polo brothers helped facilitate travel between West and East. This imaginative picture of Hangzhou in China hints at the riches found there.**

Venice was the dominant commercial state in Europe and a vital entrepôt between the East and the West in the thirteenth century, with their galleys controlling much of the trade that came through the Mediterranean. When its governing body, the Council of Ten, heard of the great Mongol empire rising in the East, they needed information on its plans and intentions. Fortunately, there was an enterprising family that already had connections in the East.

ABOVE **The Polos were not simple merchants. They were tasked by the Venetian government with gathering commercial and military intelligence. Here the family is shown leaving Venice.**

Niccolò and Maffeo Polo were Venetian traders who had a thirst for knowledge and adventure. In c. 1260 the two brothers set out on what was a routine trading visit to the Black Sea. While there they were invited to join a caravan that was destined to travel all the way from Europe to China. On this remarkable journey, the two Venetians penetrated deep into what is now known as Russia before turning south and traveling between the Aral and Caspian seas. The caravan proceeded to the exotic trading town of Bukhara, before following the northern route of the Silk Road above the Taklamakan Desert. They traveled to the south of the Gobi Desert before arriving in Beijing and the court of the Mongol ruler Kublai Khan.

Here they were welcomed by the khan, who was an open-minded man with a fascination for foreign cultures and beliefs. One of the strengths of the Mongol empire was its toleration of different religions, and within the court were representatives of the Muslim, Buddhist, and animist faiths. Kublai was interested to hear about the

ABOVE Niccolò and Maffeo Polo traveled with the blessing of Pope Gregory X.

Christian god and he invited the Polo brothers to return with 100 priests and some of the holy oil that was burnt in the lamps at the Holy Sepulchre in Jerusalem. He nominated the two men as his envoys to the pope and sent them on their way after showering them with wealth. Almost a decade after embarking on their voyage, the brothers returned to Venice.

They paused at home in Venice for a while before setting off again. This time they took Niccolò's son Marco and two friars supplied by the pope. In 1271, the party reached Jerusalem and collected the required oil. They managed to hang on to the oil for their epic journey, which began in 1272—but not so the two friars. These two holy men found the going too tough and they turned back soon after the party left for the East.

The Polos left Jerusalem for Hormuz on the Persian Gulf. Here they traversed the Iranian deserts and then proceeded into the mountainous terrain of Afghanistan. There is no doubt they would have stayed at towns founded by Alexander the Great, even though many of these sites are now deserted and filled with dust. They paused for a year in Badakhshan (an historic region of Afghanistan)—the young Marco had fallen ill—before heading through the Pamir Mountains and across the Gobi Desert. On the previous journey the Polos had skirted this feature, so it was the first time that Westerners had seen the Gobi.

On the journey they faced many perils—some real and, perhaps, some imagined. Marco told how travelers could go mad in the dreadful deserts that they had to cross. In the hot desert sun, some could be lured from the caravan by voices and even music. They would wander off in the grip of the hallucination and only come to hours later, too far from their companions and doomed to die a lonely death in the heart of the desert. For this reason, it was important that all travelers stick close together. The voices could also come at night, leading to disorientation and confusion in the morning. To avoid this hazard, before the sun set travelers would make a sign in the sand showing the direction they had to travel the next day.

The Italians finally reached the Yellow River (Huang He) in China, after two years of exhausting travel. The party was met by representatives of the khan and taken to his summer palace in Shangdu, just north of Beijing.

Here Marco struck up an instant rapport with the khan. The young Italian had a gift for languages and had picked up many of the dialects spoken on his journey across the Eurasian continent. The family became trusted members of the Imperial retinue. The brothers may have acted as military advisors while Marco was dispatched on sensitive diplomatic missions to Burma, Vietnam, and India.

Kublai Khan

BELOW The Polos are shown entering Peking. Once again, the vast distances between cultures meant that European artists had no real concept of Chinese architecture.

THE WONDER OF THE GREAT WALL

EVEN TODAY, people are skeptical about this journey, and one of the key arguments used is that Marco never mentioned the Great Wall of China. However, the khan was descended from the nomadic Mongol race and the Great Wall was built to keep him and his relatives out of China. In addition, the impressive wall we know today was largely refurbished and built during the Ming Dynasty (1368–1644) that expelled the Mongol Yuan Dynasty (from the thirteenth century to 1368).

BELOW Was it all a myth? Did Polo really visit the Yuan Empire? His ignorance of the Great Wall is sometimes used as evidence to attack his veracity.

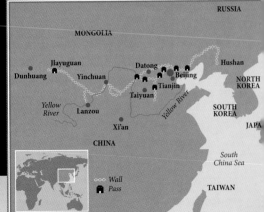

In his book, written many years after these adventures, Marco told of many wondrous things. He spoke of black rocks that were burnt to give warmth, of exploding rockets, and money that was made not of metal but of paper. He also told of the khan's mobile command headquarters, a vast palanquin mounted on the back of four armored elephants.

ABOVE Mongol leaders such as Kublai Khan were keen to show off their majesty and power. The khan rides into battle on four armored elephants.

The Travels of Marco Polo was written in approximately 1299 while Polo was confined in a Genoese jail. It was greeted with scorn by many readers who thought it was largely a work of fiction. However, some of the more bizarre stories were true. The burning rocks were of course coal, and the Mongols did use printed money. Much of what he wrote can be supported. For example, he gave an accurate description of the Mongol tribesman's diet, writing that they "subsist entirely upon flesh and milk, eating the produce of their sport ... and they eat flesh of every description, horses, camels, and even dogs, provided they are fat. They drink mare's milk which they prepare in such a manner that it has the qualities and flavor of white wine. They term it in their language *Kemurs*."

On his deathbed, Polo was asked if what he had written was true—he replied that he had only written of half the wonders he had seen. Presuming that Polo's account is accurate, he explored much of Asia in the seventeen years he stayed in the service of the khan. The Polo family had become wealthy on trade and imperial favor. However, they eventually sought leave to return home to Venice. The khan was reluctant to see his trusted aides depart but agreed to the request as long as the Polos could escort a Mongol princess to Persia where she would marry his great nephew, Argun (1258–91), the Il-Khan (subordinate ruler).

Journey Home

In 1292 the Venetians set off from the Chinese port of Zaitun (Quanzhou) in a fleet of fourteen ships with 600 crewmen. They traversed the South China Sea and made landfall on the coast of modern-day Vietnam. Skirting the mighty Khmer empire of Cambodia, the travelers crossed Malaya and went through the hazardous Strait of Malacca before visiting the wild jungles of Sumatra. Crossing the Bay of Bengal, they then visited Ceylon (Sri Lanka) and southern India before proceeding to Hormuz at the gates of the Persian Gulf. From here the family went to the Il-Khan's capital, delivered the princess, and then made their way overland back to the Mediterranean. Finally, in 1295, after twenty-four years of travel, Marco Polo returned to Italy. Much of their wealth had been stolen en route, but the returned travelers still managed to cause quite a stir when they unpicked the lining of their clothes and produced an abundance of precious stones.

Marco Polo's tales had one major consequence—Christopher Columbus (1451–1506) on reading Polo's description of Japan and the Mongol empire, became determined to discover it for himself. He even traveled with a copy of Polo's book which he had annotated with many points of interest. Columbus, not aware of the collapse of the Mongol Empire, even wrote a short speech that he intended to present to the khan's successor when they finally got to meet!

BELOW **The remarkable sea journeys of Marco Polo through the Far East inspired Christopher Columbus to set out for the Indies—although he would go west not east.**

The Galley Versus the Caravel

Ships operating in the Mediterranean ranged from small boats with a single bank of oars to mighty *galleasses*. These huge ships were more than 150ft long and could carry up to 200 soldiers. But *galleasses* had limitations—while they could grow to a massive size in the more sheltered Mediterranean Sea, they could not venture across the Atlantic since they relied primarily on oars and were too elongated to be seaworthy.

In the late medieval period, the Portuguese developed the caravel. Not nearly as imposing as the great *galleasses*, these handy ships with their gently sloping bow and a single stern castle had two or three masts. The caravels were rigged in such a manner that they could sail into the wind. These fast, maneuverable little vessels were the ones chosen by the great explorers of the time to carry out their great voyages of exploration.

Bartolomeu Dias (c. 1450–1500), Vasco da Gama (c. 1460–1524), and Christopher Columbus all established their reputations with caravels. Columbus was particularly fond of his caravel *La Niña*, which he saw as his safest and most maneuverable vessel.

Galleys were last used in combat during the Napoleonic Wars (1803–15) by the Ottoman Navy and the Barbary Corsairs—pirates who inhabited ports on the north coast of Africa. These relics of a past age shocked the sailors of Britain and America—it's said that the galleys could be smelled up to a mile away thanks to the shocking conditions endured by the galley slaves who were shackled to their oars.

ABOVE Galleys were valuable ships in the Mediterranean. However, their shallow draft and long hulls made them unsuitable for oceanic voyages.

IBN BATTUTA—NEVER TAKE THE SAME ROAD TWICE

For more than two decades, Ibn Battuta (1304–77) traveled around the world, covering an estimated 75,000 miles. He explored most of the Arabic territories and through Africa, the Middle East, and most of the Silk Road, and also journeyed deep into Asia. No doubt part of this success was due to his motto: "Never take the same road twice."

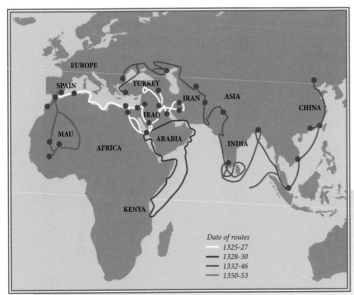

LEFT AND BELOW **Ibn Battuta's journeys rivaled those of Marco Polo—he originally set out to visit as many Islamic countries as possible. He too crossed the Silk Road. These below are the ancient ruins of Jaohe near Turpan City, Xinjiang, China.**

Date of routes
— 1325-27
— 1328-30
— 1332-46
— 1350-53

Ibn Battuta was heir to hundreds of years of Arab exploration, and the routes established by his predecessors made his journeys possible. The Indian Ocean could almost have been termed an Arabic lake. For many centuries, Arab merchants had used the monsoon to propel their trading ships eastward from the Persian Gulf in November before returning with the westward winds in summer. In the eighth century CE, Arab traders first discovered the sea route to Canton that traveled along the Malabar Coast and through the Strait of Malacca between modern-day Indonesia and Malaysia, before stopping off in Hanoi. Once the explorers reached Canton (modern day Guangzhou) the Arabs traded iron, wool, gold, and incense in return for silk and spices. Eventually the Arabs penetrated into Southeast Asia and even to Madagascar, where they established a lively trade with the Malay merchants.

Ibn Battuta's full name was Abu Abd Allah Muhummad ibn Abd Allah al-Lawati al-Tanji Ibn Battuta and he came from a privileged background. In around 1304 he was born into a respected family of judges in Tangier, Morocco. At the age of twenty-one he set off on the *hajj*—the pilgrimage that every good Muslim is required to undertake to the holy city of Mecca. Originally, Battuta was to return to Tangier and resume his career in Islamic law, but instead he was bitten by the travel bug— badly bitten.

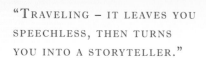

"TRAVELING – IT LEAVES YOU
SPEECHLESS, THEN TURNS
YOU INTO A STORYTELLER."
—IBN BATTUTA

On the way to Mecca, the young man had traveled eastward along the Mediterranean coast to Egypt, but got diverted southward along the Nile. From there, he went on to the Red Sea before taking a long route to Mecca that included a trip to Damascus in Syria. From Mecca he proceeded to Basra and followed the Euphrates River to Baghdad. Returning north on the Tigris, he visited Turkey before making another journey to Mecca. After he spent several years honing his skills as a scholar, his itchy feet took over—and in 1330 he founded an expedition to explore East Africa. Sailing through the Red Sea and into the Indian Ocean, Ibn Battuta and his companions reached as far as Mombasa in modern-day Kenya and Kilwa, now a town in Tanzania. While south of the equator, Battuta was impressed by the magnificent architecture of the locals.

After his African sojourn, Battuta decided to visit India—where he heard that a sultan welcomed learned travelers to his court. Rather than retracing his steps, Battuta decided to take the convoluted northern route to India.

Convoluted is something of an understatement. Once again going through Mecca, he made his way through central Turkey to Sinop on the Black Sea. The

Moroccan crossed this body of water and traversed much of the Caucasus. He traveled up the frozen Volga River (surely quite a sight for a citizen of Morocco), before returning to Turkey and Constantinople. Battuta had originally sworn to only visit Islamic lands, but he obviously discarded his initial intention. From the capital of the Byzantine empire, he resumed his travels on part of the Silk Road and went past the Caspian and Aral seas before reaching Bukhara and entering India in September 1333.

LEFT **Like many before and after, Ibn Battuta was amazed at the ruins left by the Ancient Egyptians.**

On to India

Battuta proceeded to Delhi, where he was employed by Sultan Mohammed bin Tughluq (1290–1351), the second sultan of the Tughluq dynasty. The sultan must have been delighted to have such a learned man in his court, as he honored the Moroccan with a hefty wage, estates, and the important role of chief judge over Delhi. This sinecure obviously appealed to the footloose traveler as he resided in this splendid city for seven years.

In 1341 the sultan gave the Moroccan a new assignment—maybe he recognized that his companion would soon be looking for fresh shores to conquer. Bin Tughluq ordered Battuta to lead a diplomatic mission to Beijing as his envoy to the Chinese emperor.

The sultan couldn't have made a better choice, for Battuta proved a most determined traveler—refusing to give up on the mission even though he suffered so many misfortunes on the journey that a lesser man would have abandoned the task. The first expedition was attacked by rebel Indians and most of the caravan was destroyed. The second attempt was just as bad. The envoys left Delhi and

journeyed on land to the port of Calicut, arguably the richest port in the world at the time. All of the provisions were loaded on board a fleet of dhows and the devout Muslim repaired to a mosque to pray for the success of the operation. While he was praying, a savage storm swept through the Arabian Sea and apparently destroyed two of the three ships in his fleet.

Not wanting to face his superior with the news, Battuta traveled from Calicut to the Maldives Islands and then onto Ceylon (Sri Lanka). Determined to make one last desperate attempt to fulfill his mission, he sailed up the east coast of India into Bengal

RIGHT **Sultan Mohammed bin Tughluq was a powerful patron of the visiting traveler. He respected Battuta's understanding of Islamic law.**

AFTER THE STORM, BATTUTA MANAGED TO JOIN ANOTHER SHIP
WHICH WAS ATTACKED BY PIRATES AT NIGHT: "THEY SEIZED THE
JEWELS AND RUBIES WHICH THE KING OF CEYLON HAD GIVEN ME AND
ROBBED ME OF MY CLOTHES AND PROVISIONS WITH WHICH PIOUS
[HOLY] MEN AND SAINTS HAD FAVORED ME. THEY LEFT
NOTHING ON MY BODY EXCEPT MY TROUSERS."

—IBN BATTUTA

and Assam (Myanmar) before sailing south again along the Malay Peninsula to Sumatra (Indonesia). A kind king furnished the envoy with a new junk, and after seventy-one days sailing across the South China Sea, Battuta made landfall in Quanzhou in China. The party then traveled overland until it finally reached Beijing. He was four years late. But at least he got there.

It seems that for once in his much-traveled life, while staying in China, the explorer found it difficult to deal with a foreign society. Many travelers go through episodes in which they are unable to leave their accommodation in a foreign land due to some kind of unnamed dread, and in Beijing the local love of statues and shrines caused some kind of unreasoning panic in Ibn Battuta's mind. As he wrote in the best-selling journal of his travels, *Rihla*, he stayed all day in his quarters and only left them when absolutely necessary. The Chinese use of symbols and statues in their religious practices is quite the opposite of Muslim ceremonies and this may have played a part in the Arab's feelings of alienation and isolation.

As soon as he could Battuta finished his duties as the Sultan's emissary and left China. He returned home along the coast of the Indian Ocean, going up through Persia and into Syria in 1348. Here he witnessed the dreadful effects of the bubonic plague, which had originated in China and Burma before it traveled along the Silk Road to strike Europe and the Middle East. In 1349 he returned to Morocco at the age of forty-five.

Of course, he only stayed at home for a year before crossing over the Mediterranean to Granada in Spain. Then in 1351, the Sultan of Morocco sent him on an expedition to the Mali empire in the African interior. Battuta spent several years traversing the Sahara Desert, an extremely unpleasant experience, and resided in the twin capitals of Timbuktu and Gao. It is interesting to note that Arabic travelers were well acquainted with the city of Timbuktu hundreds of years before Europeans finally reached this fabled destination.

No doubt the years were finally catching up with Ibn Battuta and in 1353 he returned to Morocco for the last time. It was here that he completed his travelogue the *Rihla* and ended his professional life as he had began, as a judge.

Hundreds of years later, a most unusual explorer followed in Ibn Battuta's footsteps. American geographer Fanny Bullock Workman (1859–1925) covered much of North Africa, Asia and penetrated deep into the Himalayas near the Silk Road on her favorite device—a single-speed bicycle. Like Battuta, Fanny and her husband, William, wrote informative travelogues of their explorations.

ABOVE **Fanny Bullock Workman, in 1905, the year she became the second-ever woman to address the Royal Geographical Society.**

Arab Slavery

Ibn Battuta had to be careful when traveling through Africa. The trade in African slaves by Arabs was well established and Africans were justifyably wary of any Arabic visitors.

Starting in about 600 CE, the Arabs had explored much of the Sahara Desert and its surrounding lands, as well as the west coast of Africa. Here they entered into a lively trade with local potentates in human flesh—and established long trade routes. Many Africans were seized in Central Africa before being delivered to towns such as Timbuktu and then marched in long, misery-filled caravans across the Sahara Desert to trading hubs in North Africa, such as Marrakech, Tunis, and Cairo. Others were collected on the east coast of Africa in towns such as Mogadishu and Zanzibar. Most of these slaves were transported in Arab dhows to Arabia, India, and even as far as China—where it was fashionable to have an African slave in your household.

The slaves endured terrible conditions. Many Arab writers tell of the skeletons lining the trading routes that went through the heart of the Sahara. If they could not keep up with the caravan they were left to die of thirst and exposure.

Estimates suggest that as many as 5,000 slaves were taken from Africa each year to be sold to both Arabic and Western owners. With the opening up of the New World by the Spanish in the sixteenth century, and the subsequent need for slave labor in the Caribbean, demand soared and tens of thousands of slaves were taken each year for the transatlantic slave trade.

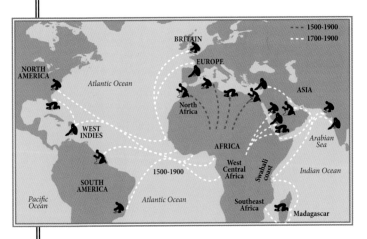

LEFT **Slavery was a curse to inhabitants of Africa. Potentates and kings came to rely on the foul trade to maintain power and purchase weapons.**

ZHENG HE

In 1401, the Chinese imperial government was determinedly isolationist and did not have a department of foreign affairs. Such an attitude persisted because it was believed that the emperor of the Celestial Kingdom was seen as the divine ruler of the entire world! Therefore there were no independent kingdoms, and so as far as the Chinese were concerned the whole world all owed allegiance to the government in Beijing.

Zheng He (c. 1371–1433) was sent out by his emperor to force obedience to the imperial will and discover new lands. The massive fleets he commanded dwarfed those of all other voyages of exploration.

In 1402, Zhu Di (1360–1424) became the third emperor of the Ming Dynasty and immediately attempted to increase the prestige of the Chinese empire. As a prince, Zhu Di had proved a doughty warrior against the Mongols whom the Ming had ejected from China in 1368.

The new emperor noticed how efficient Zheng He was and promoted his protégé to be chief eunuch of the Ming court. Zheng He was placed in charge of buildings and works in the empire, and in 1403 Zhu Di promoted Zheng He to chief ambassador and admiral. Zhu Di ordered him to build a huge fleet in order to impress other kingdoms with China's grandeur while collecting taxes and treasure.

BELOW **Zheng He is not only a Chinese hero. He is respected as a great explorer in Malaysia, as this mural in Malacca testifies.**

ABOVE For many years, the great Chinese explorer Zheng He was all but forgotten. This replica of one of his treasure ships in Nanjing testifies to the renewed interest in his journeys.

The admiral set to work with a will. He had to build a fleet that would reflect the true glory of the Celestial Empire. First he built the *baoshan* treasure ships. These were massive junks that made European caravels look tiny in comparison. The treasure ships may have been up to 500ft long and 210ft wide. They had nine massive masts rigged with efficient square sales and up to four decks, complete with state rooms for officials and barracks for soldiers. The vessels were meant to be self-sufficient and had facilities to grow soy beans to make tofu: a shallow layer of soil was spread on the decks to enable simple crops to be sown. The *baoshan* had a displacement of 20,000–30,000 tons and rivaled aircraft carriers for size. How could such massive vessels survive in the open seas? The wide beam would have imparted a great deal of stability to the ships, and with experienced captains they could avoid the worst conditions at sea. The treasure ships had considerable amounts of ballast in the V-shaped hull and watertight compartments built into the frame. Floating anchors were cast over the side to add stability, while the rudder could be lowered or raised to act as a stabilizing keel.

Accompanying the fleet were up to 180 other ships tasked with performing various duties. Almost 20,000 soldiers embarked upon the journey. Their mission was to enforce the emperor's will and overawe local kings. The *machuan* horse ships carried cavalry mounts, timber for repairs, and tribute seized from the vassal states. These *machuan* were about half the size of the *baoshan*. The *liangchuan* grain ships were of a similar size and carried provisions for the sailors and soldiers: the latter were carried in the *zuochuan* troop ships. Finally, there were the more maneuverable *zhanchuan* battleships. Fast and handy, these combat craft were the smallest in the fleet but were still twice as long as Christopher Columbus's flagship the *Santa María*.

The crews, officials, sailors, and soldiers are said to have numbered 28,000. The first expedition set out in 1405 and consisted of 208 vessels including sixty-two treasure ships. This voyage first stopped in Hue, the capital of Đàng Trong (modern Vietnam), before proceeding to the Spice Islands of Indonesia and Malaysia. Calicut in India was the furthest destination, before the fleet headed home in 1407.

Two more voyages followed, very much like the first. Local rulers were feted and given precious gifts, and "invited" to give tribute to the emperor. The fourth voyage was more spectacular still; in 1413 the fleet set off and sailed beyond India to explore the Maldives and even got as far as Hormuz on the Persian Gulf.

However, perhaps Zheng He's most spectacular voyage took place from 1417 to 1419. The fleet managed to reach the Horn of Africa and sailed along the coast as far as Kenya. Remarkable artifacts were brought back from this journey, including a giraffe for the emperor.

The final voyage of Zheng He came after Emperor Zhu Di had died. In 1431, the fleet sailed along a similar route to the first expedition, although the admiral took a detour and visited Mecca—he was a Muslim—thus performing his *Hajj* just before he died in 1433.

With the death of Zhu Di, the Ming empire turned back in on itself and the ruling class decided against further expeditions of discovery, which they argued were destabilizing the social order of the Celestial Empire. Ocean-going voyages were banned. Records and maps were burned and the mighty fleet that had explored much of the world rotted away in seaports along the Chinese coast.

RIGHT Like many eunuchs Zheng He was a trusted member of the Chinese Imperial Court. Unable to have children, they were not likely to usurp the emperor.

Did the Chinese Discover Australia and America?

Did the Chinese discover Australia? Some writers and academics believe that Zheng He's fleet continued down from Indonesia and discovered the continent of Australia hundreds of years before the first European explorers. They claim that two of his vice-admirals arrived in 1422 and spent several months exploring and looking for minerals. Hong Bao (active 1412–33) was reputed to have landed on the west coast, while Zhou Man landed on the east coast.

These theories are hotly debated, although several Chinese relics such as coins and bronze statues have been found on the Australian coast. However these could easily have come from another source. For hundreds of years, beginning in the early eighteenth century, fishermen from Sulawesi (in modern-day Indonesia) were visiting the shores of Australia to fish for sea cucumber.

These *trepangers*, as they were known, would spend several months fishing and preserving their catch before heading back to Indonesia, where they would often sell them to Chinese merchants.

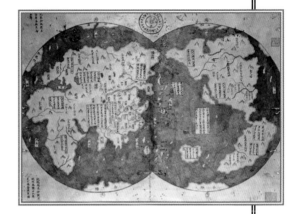

ABOVE **This map is often used as evidence that Zheng He visited Australia and America. However, it is most likely a copy of a European map.**

One piece of evidence could solve this mystery. Zheng He kept accurate maps of his travels which could have offered proof. Sadly, they were all burned on the orders of a later emperor.

Chinese mapmakers never depicted the world as two ovals joined together to represent the different hemispheres as the above reproduction does. In all probability, the artifact is a copy of a nineteenth-century European map rather than the copy of a fifteenth-century Chinese map.

Sea cucumber fished by the Sulawesi fishermen

USHERING IN THE NEW WORLD—
PRINCE HENRY THE NAVIGATOR

For medieval seafarers one location struck fear into their hearts. Cape Bojador, 1,000 miles along the African coast from Gibraltar, pokes into the Atlantic Ocean. At the western edge of the vast Sahara Desert, the sandy and rocky wastes meet huge rollers thundering in from the Atlantic. A shallow underwater platform extends miles out from the Cape, threatening any ships that come too close with ruination. It was known to swallow ships whole.

Terrible tales were told of this location. The heat from the sun was so fierce that waterproof pitch would melt away and sailors' skin would turn black. Terrible monsters lurked in the shadows waiting to clutch even the largest ships in their maws and drag the luckless crews deep down into their undersea lairs. Navigators might try to skirt the dangers by sailing far out to sea, but there they faced the danger of plummeting off the edge of the world.

Prince Henry
of Portugal

Cape Bojador was a physical and psychological barrier to European exploration, but one man was determined to break through it. Prince Henry of Portugal laid the foundations for European oceanic exploration. He was born to John I of Portugal (reigned 1385–1433) and Philippa of Lancaster (1360–1415). Portugal was nearly bankrupt after many years of warfare and strife. The small kingdom was surrounded by the rising Spanish kingdom and the Atlantic Ocean, so if the country was to grow and become more powerful it needed to look overseas.

BELOW **The Portuguese are justly proud of their early explorers. This monument that looks over the Atlantic features Henry the Navigator at the forefront of thirty-three other explorers.**

Vasco da Gama

TOP **Vasco da Gama cradles a caravel in his arms in this statue in Lisbon. The handy little ships were vital during the age of exploration.**

Henry chose the adventurer Gil Eannes to undertake an expedition to navigate south of the cape. After several failures, Eannes sailed far out to sea in 1434 and when a favorable wind came, turned back east toward the coast of Africa. He believed he had landed on a beach 100 miles beyond the terrible Cape Bojador, but this was probably just the already-navigated Cape Juby, around 170 miles north.

Henry went on to sponsor many expeditions. He provided enterprising sailors with the means to purchase caravels and set off in search of new lands. In 1418 and 1419, the first European oceanic colonies were founded by Portuguese explorers on both the Madeiran and Canary Islands. Another expedition penetrated far down the west coast of Africa, enabling the Portuguese to trade directly with central African states and avoid having to deal with Muslim middlemen. Portuguese mariners reached Cape Verde, Africa's westernmost point, in 1445, and when Prince Henry died in 1460 one of his expeditions was approaching Sierra Leone—2,000 miles from Portugal.

Vasco da Gama built on these foundations in 1497 when he sailed around the Cape of Good Hope and on to India—opening up the East to Portuguese trade and colonization.

The Cape Verde Islands, as well as the Azores in the mid-Atlantic, became Portuguese possessions. These island holdings became crucial stepping stones for the Spanish and Portuguese journeys across the Atlantic to the New World.

ABOVE **When Vasco da Gama's fleet reached the Indian subcontinent, he ushered in an era when Europeans would dominate much of the world.**

As well as gaining vital territory to help European expansion, Prince Henry made several other crucial contributions. The foremost shipwrights, astronomers, cartographers, sea captains, and mathematicians were enlisted to serve in his new institute for navigation and geography at the town of Sagres in the southwest of Portugal. Here his captains' newly gained knowledge of oceanic tides and wind patterns was recorded and made available for future expeditions. Here, and at the royal observatory in Lisbon, the best cartographers in Europe began piecing together an understanding of the globe and the stars above. The maps and journals of many early explorers, including Vasco Da Gama, were stored in these royal archives but sadly much material was lost in the horrific 1755 Lisbon earthquake that destroyed 85 percent of the city.

3

THE WORLD DIVIDED

WHEN CHRISTOPHER COLUMBUS (1451–1506) made landfall on an island in the Caribbean in 1492, he ushered in a period of exploration and conquest like no other. Seeking to emulate the discoveries of the Portuguese in Asia, generations of Spanish and Portuguese explorers descended on the Americas, where they penetrated into the heart of Central America, conquered the mountains and jungles of South America, and discovered the potential riches of the North American continent.

While other explorers had been motivated by curiosity and the desire to trade, the "conquistadors," as they were known, were an entirely different beast. These "conquerers" were armed with state-of-the-art weaponry and a fanatical devotion to the Christian cause.

LEFT The popes gave conquistadors such as Vasco Balboa (c. 1475–1519) God's permission to explore and conquer the Americas and Asia.

DIAS AND DA GAMA: PORTUGUESE BREAK OPEN THE WORLD

In 1482, Portuguese explorers set another precedent that would be emulated by all explorers and colonizers. A permanent settlement was established on the African coast of what is now Ghana. Elmina was founded with the assistance of a local ruler who came to rely on the military force of the new arrivals. These settlements became vital trading outposts that would fill the coffers of the founding power. The Portuguese expeditions also erected stone markers inscribed with the royal arms of Portugal when they reached new territory.

Bartolomeu Dias (c. 1450–1500) would erect several of these monuments while seeing if it was possible to navigate around the southern tip of Africa. His task was to find a new trade route to India that would bypass the routes of Arabian merchants who dominated trade to India through the Middle East. Dias sailed in August 1487 with two caravels and a supply ship.

He knew that to stick to the African coast would be nearly impossible thanks to contrary winds and difficult currents. He decided to follow the practice of previous Portuguese explorers and swing southwest out into the Atlantic Ocean, then use more favorable conditions to drive parallel to the African coast. This was accepted practice among the Portuguese explorers and had led to the discovery of Atlantic island chains such as the Azores and Madeira. When he thought they had traveled far enough Dias ordered the fleet to turn eastward and look for the African coast. None was to be found—they had overshot. He turned north and there, shimmering on the horizon, was the start of the east coast of Africa.

Dias had rounded the tip of Africa and proved that it was not connected to the South Pole. The ships made landfall at Mossel Bay before continuing north for around 250 miles, where a white cross was set up on Cape Padrone. At this point, however, his crew refused to continue on to India and threatened mutiny. Dias was forced to turn back and the expedition headed south. On the return journey they surmounted the challenge of navigating the dangerous tip of Africa. This terrifying ordeal led to Dias naming this hazardous feature the Cape of Storms.

BELOW **Wherever Bartolomeu Dias explored, he left stone columns topped with a cross to proclaim the majesty of the Portuguese throne.**

After a journey of fifteen months and 16,000 miles, the ships returned to Lisbon to the ecstatic welcome of the population. King John II (reigned 1481–95) immediately began planning another expedition, determined to reach India and dominate the European spice trade.

ABOVE **Dias's small flotilla was the first to negotiate the fierce conditions at the tip of the African continent. Many others would founder and be lost forever.**

This determination bore fruit for John's successor, Manuel I (reigned 1495–1521). On May 20, 1498, a Portuguese flotilla docked in the busy port of Calicut (modern Kozhikode). The fleet of four vessels belonging to Vasco da Gama (c. 1460–1524) had been traveling since July the previous year and had a lucky breakthrough while passing the coast of modern-day Kenya, when they recruited an experienced Muslim pilot to guide them to the Indian coast.

Calicut stunned the newly arrived Europeans. This port on what later became the border of the Mughal empire was packed with as many as 700 ships from what seemed to be every corner of the globe. Tamils, Persians, and Arabs competed with Chinese and Malays for the best prices. New spices unknown in Europe and a vast menagerie of exotic species were available for sale. Hindus and Muslims lived side by side, while it seemed to the Portuguese sailors that every second person wore an outlandish outfit or spoke a strange, incomprehensible dialect. At first the Portuguese with their meager goods seemed like poor cousins to the locals, but after several expeditions they imposed their will on the market. On a return journey in 1502 with a fleet of twenty warships, da Gama terrorized settlements on the Indian coast and won trading concessions that favored Portuguese merchants. By the time da Gama died in 1524, Portuguese settlements dotted the coastlines of India and Africa. Fortifications controlled the straits of Malacca and the Spice Islands (the modern Maluku Islands, called the Spice Islands in the sixteenth century because cloves, mace, and nutmeg were found there), as well as myriad other trading spots.

The largest country in South America was seized by the Portuguese almost by accident. Pedro Álvares Cabral (1467–1520) set off in da Gama's footsteps but went too far east when swinging through the Atlantic, and landed on the coast of what is now Brazil. He promptly appropriated this vast nation for the Portuguese crown.

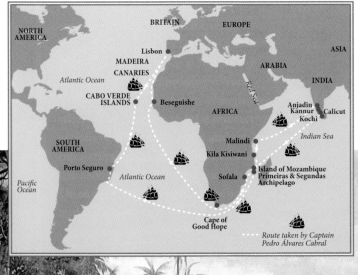

LEFT AND BELOW While some Portuguese explorers proceeded directly to the Indies, Pedro Álvares Cabral made landfall in South America and claimed the vast territory of Brazil.

CHRISTOPHER COLUMBUS

Several of the explorers in this book faced myriad challenges before they even set off on their voyages of discovery. Christopher Columbus was no exception. His plan to cross the Atlantic Ocean to find a direct route to the Spice Islands and India was rejected many times. But once he gained support from Queen Isabella of Castille (reigned 1474–1504)—in what would become Spain, once Isabella united with her husband's country, Aragon—there was no holding the explorer back and he made four journeys to the Americas in 1492, 1493, 1498, and 1502.

Even from an early age Columbus had a remarkable adventure-filled life. He was born in Genoa, the son of a wool merchant. While the profession of wool merchant might seem staid, it would have involved making and visiting contacts throughout the Mediterranean and even as far afield as the British Isles.

Columbus evidently had a thirst for adventure and from a young age he took up a position on a merchant ship. In 1476, the vessel was attacked by French privateers who seized the cargo and

BELOW **Christopher Columbus brought fabulous items back to show Ferdinand and Isabella of Spain—but where were the gold and spices?**

scuttled the boat while it was sailing off the Portuguese coast. Columbus floated to shore on a piece of timber, lucky to survive the ordeal. Fortune favors the brave: Columbus took advantage of his circumstances to make his way to Lisbon where he immersed himself in the latest teachings that pertained to seafaring and exploration, including mathematics, astronomy, cartography, and navigation. During this period, it appears that Columbus visited England and Iceland. In Bristol the seaman witnessed the 50ft tides common on the coast of that part of south west England—these hinted at the size of the ocean before him. While visiting Iceland he perhaps heard tales of a new world discovered by ancient Norse explorers.

Christopher Columbus

While in Portugal, Columbus came into the orbit of the mathematician Paolo dal Pozzo Toscanelli (1397–1482). This influential teacher made a vital contribution to Columbus's voyage—by making a colossal mistake. Using the latest mathematics, Toscanelli and his school sought to estimate the circumference of the globe. Most of their calculations had some grounding in reality, but they made one crucial mistake. They underestimated the circumference by one quarter—the best brains in the business managed to chop out the bit of the Earth just where the American continents were. When Columbus set sail he was confident that after traveling a certain distance he would end up bumping into Asia and the subcontinent.

Columbus pitched his idea to sail westward to the rulers of Portugal and England but they were not interested; however, Spain's rulers Ferdinand (reigned 1479–1516) and Isabella were. Seeking to rival the riches and glory of their Portuguese neighbors, they embraced the Genoan adventurer's plan and financed the expedition. Columbus would be able to keep 10 percent of any booty and would be given a noble title and the governorship of any new lands.

With a letter to the Chinese emperor and an Arab translator fluent in several eastern languages, Columbus set out on his epic journey on August 3, 1492.

During the early morning of October 12, 1492, Columbus saw something on the horizon. As he gazed out over the prow of his flagship, the *Niña*, he witnessed a strange sight like "a little wax candle rising and falling." Four hours later, the experienced sailor Rodrigo de Triana (born 1469), was the first to sight the Americas from the forecastle of the *Pinta*.

Niña

It had been a close-run thing. A few days earlier, Columbus faced a revolt from crewmembers terrified that unfavorable easterly winds would make it impossible to make a return journey to their homelands in Europe. Fortunately, plants and sticks floating in the water demonstrated that they had almost reached their destination— and the fleet pressed on.

As dawn brightened into day, the flotilla sailed into a little bay of Watling Island in the Bahamas. In two short months, Columbus and his crew sailing the *Niña*, the *Pinta*, and the *Santa María*, had crossed the Atlantic. Columbus was rowed ashore, the island was christened San Salvador, and it was declared a possession of the Spanish crown. Small trinkets were given to some watching natives who would have had trouble making sense of the remarkable figures, clad in leather and iron, who had turned up on their doorstep.

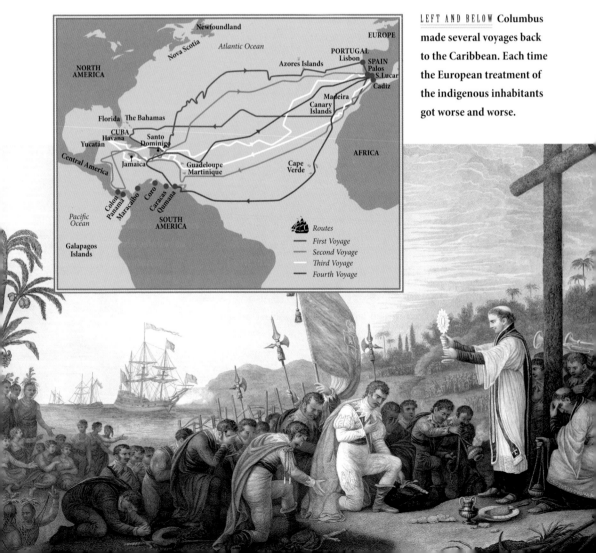

LEFT AND BELOW **Columbus made several voyages back to the Caribbean. Each time the European treatment of the indigenous inhabitants got worse and worse.**

This first cultural contact between the two peoples was harmonious—even joyful. For the rest of the day the locals, called the Taínos, played around the three ships, frolicking in canoes, and bringing fresh fruit, which was exchanged for beads and more trinkets. Columbus wrote of an overwhelming joy, not only due to the satisfaction of safely reaching land but also to the innocence and simplicity of the people he had encountered.

There was one cause for concern. The Arab translator, who was fluent in several eastern languages including Chinese, could make neither head nor tail of the local language.

This concern turned to disquiet during the next few months when Columbus sailed from island to island looking for the riches he had to take back to his Spanish patrons. Uppermost in Columbus's mind was the knowledge that his journey of exploration was primarily a commercial enterprise. Upon docking on Hispaniola, he finally had to come to grips with the fact that there was no vast trading entrepôt in these waters. The fabled lions, tigers, elephants, and camels that populated the Indian subcontinent, and the mighty empires rich in spice, silk, and precious metals with which he could trade, were not there. They did, however, come across some new peoples, including the fierce Caribs, after whom the Caribbean was named.

The commercial imperative of Columbus's mission would not be fulfilled. Things took a turn for the worse on Christmas Day, 1492. The *Santa María* drifted into a coral reef and was wrecked. Timber from the stricken ship was hauled ashore and used to build the first European settlement in Central America: La Navidad. The settlement was inhabited by members of *Santa María*'s crew, alongside the friendly locals, while the rest of the expedition sailed for home.

This happy coexistence between cultures did not last long. When the diminished flotilla embarked upon its return journey in January 1493, the forty crewmen left behind in La Navidad demonstrated their capacity for brutality. Women were abused, gold stolen; to the amazement of the Taínos, each Spaniard ate in a day what the locals consumed in a week, even though they refused to eat the little dogs raised by the Taínos for the table.

When Columbus returned to the islands in November 1493, it was not to explore but to invade. Seventeen ships and 1,300 men, including soldiers and settlers, found La Navidad burned to the ground. Hundreds of the local tribespeople were enslaved by the returning Spaniards and forced to rebuild the settlement,

BELOW **When the Europeans first arrived at Hispaniola they were enchanted by the simple life lived by the locals—it was like a new Garden of Eden.**

which was renamed Isabella, under the watchful eye of Columbus's brothers Bartolomeo and Diego. Using war dogs and mounted lancers, the Spanish swept through the island capturing thousands more. Unable to send gold to his royal masters, the admiral sent 550 captives to Spain as slaves. Half died on the way and the rest were sent back by a horrified Isabella. Most of these perished, too.

In May 1498, Columbus set sail from Spain for his third voyage and broke new ground as an explorer. Trinidad and the South American mainland were mapped. But when he returned to Isabella he found a dire situation, with colonists and natives engaged in pitched battles against each other.

A fourth expedition took Columbus to the narrow isthmus of Panama. The indigenous residents now knew what the Spanish were likely to do and this flotilla was attacked: two of the four ships were seized and destroyed. Columbus returned to Spain, broken and broke, to see out his days until he died in 1506 in a small house in Valladolid.

Whenever one thinks of great explorers, the name of Christopher Columbus comes to mind. Sadly, he must also be remembered for setting a bloody precedent for later explorers—exploitation, slavery, and murder. Columbus began the process that would see the indigenous peoples of the Caribbean virtually wiped out in the following decades.

He never did get to deliver that letter to the emperor of China.

BELOW **The Caribs, whose name lives on in the Caribbean Sea, were relatively new arrivals to the region. The people were fierce and warlike.**

Fascinating Fact—The Cargo of the Dead

Explorers from the Catholic nations of Spain and Portugal had a desperate fear of being buried in unhallowed ground. They feared that they would be consigned to hell if they were buried in heathen lands. Many sailors who died at sea were stored in the ship's hold until they returned to Europe, where their cadavers would be reburied in church grounds. Protestant nations had a much more practical solution. Their dead were wrapped in old sail cloth with a cannon ball at their feet and consigned to the watery deep.

HERNÁN CORTÉS

Aztec emperor Montezuma II (c. 1466–1520) was of an anxious disposition. Unpopular with many of his people, he had proved to be the most tyrannical of all of the Aztec rulers. Upon coming to power, he had the entire imperial household of his predecessor executed.

By 1509, his warriors had been beaten in several wars against the neighboring Tlaxcalan. Omens of impending doom were mounting. One of his most trusted advisers warned the emperor of a cataclysmic vision he had experienced. He foretold the devastation of the Mexica cities, the death of their women and children, and the rebellion of their many vassal states. Soon after, a young priest gazed up at the midnight sky and saw a great comet approaching the Aztec capital Tenochtitlán, home to around 200,000 people. It reappeared the next evening bleeding fire like a wound in the eastern sky. Soothsayers were summoned to explain the portent of the comet, but—unable to satisfy the emperor's demands—were all executed. Temples burst into flame, lighting struck some of the Aztecs' most sacred enclosures, and Lake Texcoco, on which Tenochtitlán was founded, flooded—destroying many of the city's suburbs.

BELOW **Aztec emperor Montezuma II was prey to many fears. His gloomy disposition and fatalistic outlook helped Cortés destroy his powerful empire.**

"Indeed, hardly a day passed by that these people did not
sacrifice from three to four, and even five Indians, tearing
the hearts out of their bodies, to present them to the idols
and smear the blood on the walls of the temple. The arms and
legs of these unfortunate beings were then cut off and
devoured, just in the same way we should fetch meat from
a butcher's shop and eat it."

—Cortés

As 1519 approached, Montezuma's fear only grew further. According to mythology, the godlike figure Quetzalcoatl had sworn, 500 years before this date, that he would return and take his rightful place as ruler of Central America in precisely this year, known as 1 Reed in the Aztec calendar. He would emerge from across the sea clad in silver armor with divine weapons to destroy any usurpers. The Mexica had adopted this mythology from their Toltec forbears and Montezuma was convinced that his world would soon come to an end.

He was right.

On March 4, 1519, Hernán Cortés landed on the coast of Central America at Veracruz. Strong-willed, ruthless, and filled with a lust for gold, the conquistador scuttled his own boats in order to make sure his men didn't mutiny and try to return home, and headed inland bent on conquest.

As the Spanish marched into the interior, they were impressed by the richness of the land and the well-built city-states they encountered. Fields of maize were interspersed with plantations bearing all kinds of tropical fruit and spices. The population appeared well fed and content.

The center of each city or town featured a stepped pyramid or altar. As the Spanish inspected these structures, they soon realized that the Aztec empire was built on human sacrifices.

Cortés wrote: "They have a most horrid and abominable custom which truly ought to be punished and which until now we have seen in no other part, and this is that, whenever they wish to ask something of their idols, in order that their plea may find more acceptance, they take many girls and boys and even adults, and in the presence of these idols they open their chests while they are still alive and take out their hearts and entrails and burn them before the idols, offering the smoke as sacrifice. Some of us have seen this, and they say it is the most terrible and frightful thing they have ever witnessed."

Veteran conquistador Bernal Díaz del Castillo (c. 1495– 1584) left a detailed account of all that was witnessed in his two-volume book *The Conquest of New Spain*. As soon as they landed, according to Díaz, they came upon a temple dedicated to Tezcatlipoca that still reeked of the blood of two boys who had had their hearts cut out that very day.

RIGHT The Aztecs had many gods and almost all required regular bloody sacrifices, which took place throughout the year. Men, women, children, guinea pigs—none were safe.

Tezcatlipoca

Farming of human flesh almost reached an industrial scale, as Díaz reported of the goings on in Cholula, Mexico's second city: "I … must add a word or two about the wooden cages we saw in this town. These were constructed of heavy timber, and filled with grown-up men and little boys, who were fattening there for the sacrifices and feasts. These diabolical cages Cortés ordered to be pulled down, and sent the prisoners each to their several homes."

At the Great Temple that sat at the heart of the Aztec capital Tenochtitlán, human sacrifice was conducted on a colossal scale. When the temple was dedicated, it is thought that as many as 80,000 individuals were sacrificed over a three-day period.

When relations between the Aztec and Cortés broke down, around seventy Spanish soldiers were captured and sacrificed atop this bloody temple.

Díaz witnessed their deaths—surely the worst fate suffered by any conquistador: "We could plainly see the platform, with the chapel in which those cursed idols stood; how the Mexicans … compelled their victims to dance round the god Huitzilopochtli; we saw how they stretched them out at full length on a large stone, ripped open their breasts with flint knives, tore out the palpitating

BELOW Each city in Central America had its own temples for the sacrifice of humans. The victim's remains were eaten or left to rot.

heart, and offered it to their idols. Alas! we were forced to be spectators of all this, and how they then seized hold of the dead bodies by the legs and threw them headlong down the steps of the temple, at the bottom of which other executioners stood ready to receive them, who severed the arms, legs, and heads from the bodies, drew the skin off the faces, which were tanned with the beards still adhering to them, and produced as spectacles of mockery and derision at their feasts; the legs, arms, and other parts of the body being cut up and devoured!"

But all of this was in the future. In 1519, the conquistadors marched into the heart of the Aztec empire.

Many tribes—including the fierce Tlaxcalan, who had never been subdued by the Aztecs— tried to stop the march, and Cortés' army of approximately 600 men fought several pitched battles. Cortés had caught several female translators while on earlier expeditions in the Yucatán Peninsula and used these intermediaries to argue that he was there to free the subject peoples from the bloodthirsty tyrants— the Aztecs. This strategy paid off and soon many seasoned warriors joined the Spanish expeditionary force.

ABOVE Montezuma was succeeded by more warlike emperors. But Spanish allies and European diseases eventually destroyed the Aztec state.

In November 1519, Cortés—his army swollen with thousands of Tlaxcalan auxiliaries—approached Tenochtitlán. All of the conquistadors were amazed at the beauty of the city, which more than rivaled any European capital. Its population of 200,000 lived among canals and islands that produced a rich harvest. On the larger islands, sumptuous palaces sat alongside impressive temples, all whitewashed and gleaming in the tropical sun. In Europe, only Naples and Paris had similar-sized populations at this time.

Sure that the Spaniards were divine, Montezuma did not set his army against the invaders, instead choosing to greet them with gifts and offerings when he met them on November 8. But he had let a serpent into his midst—and one week later Cortés arrested the emperor. Montezuma refused to order his commanders to attack the Spanish and it was only after several Spanish massacres and atrocities that the Aztec population rose up and expelled the invaders from their capital.

On June 30–July 1, 1520, during the aptly named "Night of Sorrows," the Spaniards were chased out of Tenochtitlán. An estimated 450 Spaniards and their allies were killed and their cannon and treasure captured by the triumphant Aztecs.

In the chaos, Montezuma was killed and a new Aztec emperor installed to resist a Spanish counterattack. This was not long in coming and in April and May 1521 reinvigorated Spanish forces assaulted the city. They also had one great ally— smallpox (see box, page 98)—which decimated their opposition.

Finally, in August 1521, the last resistance was crushed. The once beautiful city of Tenochtitlán was reduced to a blazing, blood-soaked ruin, with tens of thousands of bodies choking the streets or rotting in the canals.

Cortés named the bloody ruin Mexico City and ruled it as governor for several years. One of his first acts was to destroy the Great Temple, in which so many people were sacrificed on its altars, and to use the materials to build a cathedral.

In less than a decade, the Spanish would conduct their own human sacrifices in Mexico City when the Inquisition staged their **BELOW One of the Spaniard's** first *auto-da-fés* —the ritualized burning of heretics at the stake.

first acts was to destroy the

Great Temple and use its stones Cortés' career of exploration was not over. He also explored

to build a Christian cathedral. Central America, traveling through Honduras, and went north to the Gulf of California.

Opening and Naming the Amazon

Tales of the mythical South American city of El Dorado entranced European conquistadors. Spanish adventurer Francisco de Orellana (1511–46), convinced that the city lay somewhere in the vast reaches of the Amazon jungle, was the first European to traverse the mighty Amazon River. De Orellana set out in February 1541 from Quito under the command of Francisco Pizarro (c. 1471–1541). The impressive expedition involved around 300 Spaniards and 4,000 native bearers.

ABOVE The Amazon River and its vast drainage basin is still a land of danger and mystery. Many explorers lost their lives there searching for gold and riches.

Crossing the Andes proved to be immensely difficult and within a matter of months the expedition had lost more than half the men through desertion and disease. Upon leaving the mountains and reaching the headwaters of the Napo River, Pizarro ordered the construction of a brigantine and commanded De Orellana to travel downstream to scout out the terrain and return within the week.

In the event, returning proved impossible, thanks to the swift current, so De Orellana and his fifty men continued down to the confluence with the Amazon River, reaching the mighty waterway in June 1542. By this time Pizarro had given up waiting and returned to Quito with only 80 survivors.

The river expedition faced many dangers from giant anacondas and man-eating fish. The indigenous tribes along the way also provided quite a challenge to the Spanish: perhaps the greatest threat of all came from a people called the Pira-Tapuya who launched a savage attack on the Spanish in June. At the forefront of the attackers were the women of the tribe, who traditionally fought alongside the men. De Orellana dubbed them "Amazons"—after the mythical Amazon warriors described by ancient Greek historian Herodotus (c. 484–425 BCE) in his *Histories*—and this incident led to the naming of the entire river basin as the Amazon. He had originally named it the Rio de Orellana, but the other name stuck.

After many trials and tribulations, the expedition finally reached the open sea in August 1542.

Francisco de Orellana

Queen Isabella and The Age of Exploration

Just as Henry the Explorer sparked a golden age of Portuguese exploration, so did Isabella of Castile promote new journeys of exploration.

Isabella assumed the throne of Castile in 1474, and when she married Ferdinand II of Aragon the pair inherited a fractured kingdom. Spain was riven by internal dissent, civil war and heresy. The Muslim state of Granada refused to bow to the king and queen's authority and it took many years of bitter fighting to unite their two kingdoms. Once the *Reconquista* was complete, Isabella was aware that there was a group of unemployed conquistadors who could cause trouble for the new kingdom.

While at Santa Fe overseeing the last battle to expel the Muslims, Isabella was approached by Christopher Columbus with his proposal to reach the Indies by sailing to the west. Overcoming much resistance, the queen threw her support behind the explorer and even, it is said, swore to sell her royal jewelery to fund the expedition. While this is likely an apocryphal tale, she caused the terms for the expedition to be drawn up and ensured that Columbus had the necessary funds.

Isabella and her husband were devout Catholics and there is no doubt that the chance to spread Rome's faith to new worlds was part of the attraction of Columbus's scheme. The royal pair gave the Spanish Inquisition free reign in their domains in an attempt to root out the Jewish and Muslim faith.

Isabella could show great compassion. When Columbus sent enslaved people from the Caribbean as a gift to his royal patron, the queen was shocked and ordered that they be immediately released and sent homeward. Few survived but her concern for the rights of the indigenous inhabitants remained a preoccupation.

By the time Isabella died in 1504, she and her husband had united Spain under a powerful centralized government and half of the world had been granted to her empire with the Treaty of Tordesillas.

Queen Isabella of Castile with Ferdinand II of Aragon

LOPE DE AGUIRRE

One more Spaniard stands out as a great searcher for El Dorado. Lope de Aguirre "the Madman" (c. 1510–61) was convinced that he would find the mythical city and planned to use its wealth to carve out an empire that rivaled that of the Spanish king.

"Going troppo" is slang for a condition created by continued exposure to hot tropical climates that leads to madness and delusional fantasies. It seems that Aguirre suffered from the malady.

A minor Basque noble who arrived in the New World around 1534, Aguirre established a reputation for brutality as he joined various factions among the warring conquistadors. At the Battle of Chuquinga in 1554, he was instrumental in putting down the uprising of Francisco Hernández Girón (died 1554). Aguirre was wounded in this battle and spent the rest of his life with a crippled right leg. Giron suffered a much worse fate. His head was severed and impaled on a pole, but not before his beard and eyebrows had been shaved off and used as ornaments on the victor's hat.

In 1559, the bitter and quarrelsome warrior was attached to the expedition of Spanish conquistador Pedro de Ursúa (1526–61) to find El Dorado. The viceroy of Peru sent Aguirre to support Ursúa, but the appointment was a disaster and the 370 Spanish soldiers soon became fed up with months of fruitless searching in the Amazon while being attacked by elusive natives and ferocious insects. Capitalizing on this disenchantment, Ursúa was probably murdered by Aguirre, who then led his dwindling band of warriors down the Amazon. He then founded the new kingdom of Peru, Tierra Firme and Chile and, after killing any Spaniards of noble blood, declared himself emperor.

Continuing down the Orinoco River, Aguirre reached the sea and sacked the Spanish settlement at Isla Margarita, massacring its citizens. Aguirre then landed on the mainland at Panama where his followers were promised a full pardon if they abandoned their increasingly paranoid leader. They did desert. Alone and surrounded, Aguirre murdered his beloved daughter Elivira, so that she would not fall into his enemies' hands, before he was hacked to pieces.

ABOVE **Indigenous warriors were not the only threat to the Spanish overlords. In the bloody Battle of Chuquinga, Spanish factions fought for control of Peru's riches.**

African Conquistadors

It is a little-known fact that Africans played an important role in many of the expeditions of the conquistadors.

Some scholars think that Africans reached the Americas several centuries before Columbus. There is evidence that the ruler of the Mali empire (1230–1670) in West Africa, Mansa Abubakari, was convinced that the Atlantic Ocean was just a mighty river. In 1311 he set off at the head of a vast fleet in search of the new lands. It seems that the fleet was scattered and the emperor landed in Brazil, while other boats ended up in Mexico and even Colorado. Some aspects of African culture may have still existed when the Spanish arrived two centuries later.

Pedro Alonso Niño (c. 1468–c. 1505) was a skilled seaman and the pilot of the *Santa María* during Columbus's first voyage to the Americas in 1492. Pedro is thought to have been the son of an African slave and he was known as "el Negro." His brother Juan was at the helm of the *Niña* and was accompanied on this ship by their youngest sibling Francisco.

The brothers took part in later expeditions and such was the respect that Pedro earned for his seafaring abilities that he was entrusted with his own expedition. In 1499, they visited many islands in the Caribbean, where they amassed a fortune in pearls and other precious trade goods. Upon returning to Spain, King Ferdinand II had Pedro imprisoned in the belief that the explorer had not turned over the correct amount of the spoils. Pedro died in prison before his trial could take place.

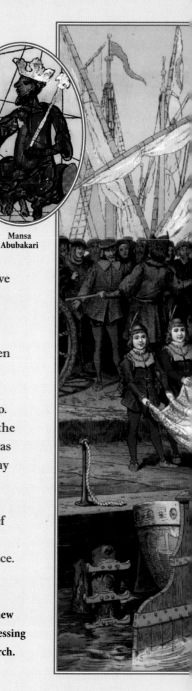

Mansa
Abubakari

RIGHT When Columbus set off to find a new route to the Indies, he did so with the blessing of Spanish royalty and the Catholic Church. Some Africans were on his crew.

HORSES, STEEL, AND GUNPOWDER

A vast gulf separated the military technology of the conquistadors from that of the peoples they sought to conquer. None exploited this superiority more effectively than Francisco Pizarro.

Pizarro typified the hard-bitten conquistadors who explored the New World. Born in around 1471 in Spain, he was the bastard son of an infantry colonel. In 1502, Pizarro joined the stream of ambitious soldiers heading to the New World and spent the next two decades exploring and seeking his fortune. He was Vasco Núñez de Balboa's (1475–1519) second in command when the Spanish first reached the Pacific. In subsequent travels, Pizarro encountered the gold-rich Incas.

Pizarro decided to take their empire for himself. In January 1531, he set sail from Panama City south along the Pacific coast. With a tiny force of 180 men, he disembarked at a point in Peru that was given the name San Miguel.

Even though there were only 180 men, they were at the forefront of a military system that dominated Europe and the Americas. The foot soldiers wore practical morion helmets, breastplates, arm- and leg-greaves, and a coat of chain mail. Made of the finest steel, this carapace was proof against most of the indigenous stone and wooden weapons. The Spaniards were also heavily armed. Each man had a sword made of the finest Toledo steel and dirks for close-in work. Many indigenous peoples were terrified of horses and dozens of lance-armed cavaliers could go through enemy formations like a hot knife through butter. Finally, Pizarro had a squad of harquebusiers and four light cannon. Lead shot from the guns and canister shot from the cannon terrified and decimated indigenous warriors.

Pizarro marched into the heart of the empire and demanded an audience with Atahuallpa, the Inca emperor (reigned 1532–33). The ruler of an empire stretching for 1,000 miles and made up of at least 12 million subjects met the adventurers at the city of Cajamarca.

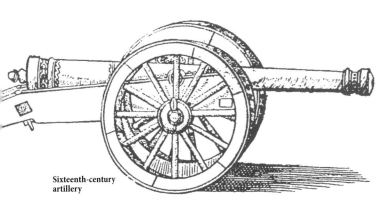

Sixteenth-century artillery

LEFT **Uniforms made from cloth, feathers or skins could not stand up against the cannons deployed by the Spanish. Grape shot and ball rendered the indigenous darts and arrows obsolete.**

On November 15, 1532, the Inca with 7,000 retainers filed into the town square. At a given signal Pizarro's men attacked the retinue. Lead balls smashed into many of the Inca nobility and the canister-loaded cannon cut bloody swathes through the tightly packed warriors. Horsemen broke into the square, routing hundreds in a deadly stumbling panic. Those who did manage to fight back found that their stone clubs or wooden spears could bruise the conquistadors but could not inflict a fatal wound. The Inca mode of battle was highly ritualized and often conducted at long range whereas the Spanish closed in for the kill with a quick, deadly thrust of Spanish steel.

ABOVE The Andes Mountains were no barrier to Pizarro's ruthless ambitions. Horses were the Spaniards' secret weapons that could put whole armies to flight.

When the swordsmen reached Atahuallpa's litter, they sought to cut down the bearers and capture the emperor. The royal attendants resisted in the only way they could—even as their hands were lopped off they desperately tried to hold up the bier with bloody stumps. Finally, Atahuallpa tumbled to the ground and was captured. Most of the Inca army's officers had been killed in the massacre and their army broke before fleeing into the hills.

Pizarro kept Atahuallpa as a hostage and demanded a ransom of a room filled with gold. For eight months, the riches of the huge empire poured into Spanish arms. When the bargain was fulfilled on July 26, 1533, Pizarro broke his word and executed his helpless captive.

BELOW At the battle of Cajamarca the Incas had not a chance against the combined arms of the seasoned Spanish conquistadors. Thousands of innocent people were massacred.

The ruthless conquistador used his share of the gold to hire more troops, and in the following year moved to capture the Inca capital at Cuzco. To all intents and purposes his devastating use of a very small force of soldiers at the Battle of Cajamarca had already won him the largest empire in South America.

Inca Human Sacrifice

As the conquistadors penetrated into the Inca empire they probably did not notice the small cairns of stones by the roadways or on the mountaintops that line the main routes to Cusco. These were small shrines used by the Incas to mark the limits of their empire and within which were the preserved bodies of young children killed as human sacrifices. The children were selected by local administrators for their beauty and treated like royalty for a year. After this they were sacrificed by their handlers strangling them or forcing them to take a fatal dose of drugs. The dead children were then placed as sentinels on the Inca borders to protect the empire from hostile incursions.

ABOVE **The last vestiges of the Inca Empire managed to hold out for several decades against the Spanish by retreating to hideaways high in the Andes.**

RIGHT **At all corners of the Inca Empire, the most beautiful and gifted children were sacrificed to the gods and placed in cairns to mark the empire's borders.**

MAGELLAN—THE FAILED CONQUISTADOR

Ferdinand Magellan (c. 1480–1521) may have been a great explorer, but he was an inept conquistador. He paid for it with his life. Born into a minor Portuguese family, Magellan's early life was filled with adventure, although he was wounded in battle and walked with a limp. In 1517 he sought support from Portugal's King Manuel I to find a route to the Spice Islands by sailing westward past the American continents rather than the usual way of traveling eastward around Africa. Manuel refused but the Spanish king, Charles I (reigned 1516–58), agreed, hoping that he would profit from the new route.

The Spanish knew that an entirely new ocean existed on the other side of the Americas thanks to the efforts of Vasco Núñez de Balboa. This explorer made the greatest real-estate grab in history when he "took possession" of the entire Pacific Ocean for his emperor!

BELOW Ferdinand Magellan's expedition was the first to circumnavigate the world. Here he arrives in the Philippines where he thought Christianity and Spanish steel would guarantee victory.

Balboa had a chequered career. He crept into a ship as a stowaway to get to the New World in an attempt to escape crippling debts. He soon proved his mettle and carved out a new Spanish colony on the Atlantic shore of what is now Panama. The Spaniard founded the first permanent European settlement on the South American mainland in 1510—Santa Maria la Antigua del Darién.

In 1513, searching for a lost kingdom and "rivers of gold," Balboa and a party of 190 conquistadors with a pack of attack dogs set off across the succession of swamps and jungles that cover the Isthmus of Panama. The Spaniards befriended locals and pressed them into battle against other tribes, also unleashing savage Spanish attack dogs. These animals, which terrified the indigenous peoples, were becoming common in many conquistador expeditions. Few natives could stand up to the dogs—and they were literally torn apart when the Spanish handlers set them onto their victims.

Climbing a mountain peak on September 25, 1513, Balboa finally saw the sight that had eluded all of the European explorers since Columbus—the vast expanse of water that we now know as the Pacific Ocean. He marched down to the shore's edge and plunged into the water, still wearing his armor. He raised his sword and took possession in the name of King Ferdinand of Aragon and his daughter Queen Joanna (1479–1555) of Castile.

ABOVE No savagery was too much for the Spanish when attacking "heathens." Here Balboa sets a pack of attack dogs onto the indigenous peoples of Central America.

Now that the Spanish monarchs knew of the ocean, they were keen to find a sea route to the Indies. Magellan's expedition was financed on the promise that he would find a southwest passage between the oceans.

On September 20, 1519, five ships and 270 crew set off. They made landfall at Rio de Janeiro and then sailed south along the coast of South America. Battling poor weather and mutiny (Magellan had one of the mutinous captains flayed alive), the fleet put in at a bay in what is now known as Patagonia. Here the Spanish invented a story about meeting a race of giants twice the height of the Europeans. However, a century later Francis Drake contradicted to this myth, noting that "they are nothing so monstrous and giant-like as they were represented, there being some English men as tall as the highest we could see."

The near subarctic environment in this bottom tip of the continent was filled with other surprises. Two islands populated by "geese" were found. These strange birds were covered all over with short black feathers, had wings that could not be used for flying, and lived entirely on fish. These were, of course, penguins—and were found in such profusion that the explorers caught enough to fill the stores of all five ships in less than an hour.

In October 1520, the fleet set off again and found what appeared to be a bay but was in fact a strait leading from the Atlantic to the Pacific. This was named the Strait of Magellan. One ship had been lost at sea, while another deserted, so Magellan and the three remaining ships set off for what they thought would be a short trip to the Spice Islands. In fact traversing the strait was no mean feat in itself. For 375 miles the flotilla wended its ways between dangerous crags and narrow gaps.

Eventually after a month confined in the straits, they finally reached the Pacific Ocean. Magellan often had trouble with his Spanish crew—after all, he was Portuguese; several times they threatened to mutiny and turn back to the Atlantic. Their captain insisted that he had charts guaranteeing they would reach their destination. This is one of the mysteries of his voyage. Some maintain that he had copies of ancient charts drawn up by Chinese navigator Admiral Zheng (1371–c. 1433)!

The ocean was calm, leading to Magellan dubbing it "the Pacific" but the journey was much longer than expected and scurvy set in to decimate the crews. After more than one hundred days at sea, the fleet made landfall at Guam in the Philippines on March 6, 1521. This new land was named the Lazarus Islands by Magellan, possibly because the fresh vegetables found there brought the starving crew back to life. For some reason this name did not stick, and they were later renamed the Philippines in honor of the Emperor Philip II (1527–98).

The friendly tribes told Magellan of the neighboring island of Matan, ruled by a fierce warrior named Lapu-Lapu who possessed a warlike and large army. The Europeans sent envoys demanding that Lapu-Lapu pledge allegiance to the Spanish crown and adopt Christianity.

When Magellan set out to impose his will on Lapu-Lapu, his subordinates urged their captain to stay behind lest he risk the expedition, but Magellan would not listen. On April 27, 1521, the conquistadors set out in three landing boats with sixty soldiers. Local allies offered 1,000 warriors in support, but Magellan refused. The raiding party arrived three hours before dawn and found that submerged rocks kept the boats 650ft from the shore.

LEFT **Lapu-Lapu was not willing to bend the knee to the Christian invaders. He inflicted a crushing blow on Magellan's men and remains a hero to the local Filipinos.**

At dawn, Magellan launched his attack. Concerned that the salt water would rust his men's armor, Magellan had ordered them to remove the greaves that protected their legs. A small band of forty-nine men reached the shore and suddenly 1,500 furious warriors emerged from the jungle and set about the Spanish.

At first, their weapons bounced off the Spanish armor, but one individual speared a conquistador's leg and brought him down. Soon all were attacking these weak spots and conquistadors began to tumble into the surf. Magellan ordered his missile troops to fire at the tribesmen, but at long range the bullets and bolts did no damage. Rather than being overawed by the gunfire, the indigenous warriors were infuriated—and redoubled their attacks on the Europeans.

Magellan was wounded by a spear thrust into his face and was prevented from drawing his sword by an injury to his arm. Finally, he was brought down in the midst of a furious band of warriors and hacked to pieces. Lapu-Lapu had lost fifteen warriors; twenty Spaniards were killed.

With Magellan dead, the survivors set off in two directions. One ship, the *Trinidada,* tried to sail back the way they had come. The other, the *Vittoria,* sailed on to the Moluccas and loaded up with cloves before setting off for Spain along the established spice route across the Indian Ocean and around Africa. The *Vittoria* finally reached Seville on September 8, 1522, with the remaining eighteen crew aboard becoming the first men to circumnavigate the globe.

BELOW **Magellan made many blunders in his last battle. Many of his men paid for their commander's hubris.**

OLD WORLD CURSE

ONE THING AIDED the conquistadors more than anything else in their expeditions in the New World—Western diseases such as smallpox and measles.

Central America's population has been estimated at approximately 20-30 million in the years before conquest. Over the next century at least 90 percent were wiped out by various factors—slavery and epidemics foremost among them. Evidence of this catastrophe has been found in ice cores taken out of Arctic ice—humanity's carbon emissions dropped significantly on this continent in the sixteenth century. A similar drop was detected when the Black Death ravaged Eurasia and Africa in the fourteenth century.

The symptoms of measles and smallpox are similar, so it is impossible to tell exactly which pathogen was most destructive as they raged throughout the Americas. An African slave named Francisco de Eguía accompanied Cortés while in the grip of smallpox. He died two weeks into the expedition but managed to transmit the disease to the indigenous inhabitants. The initial symptoms were a rash followed by headaches and a fever. Soon pustules (fluid-filled lesions) broke out all over the skin and spread until they joined together to form large suppurating sores covering the limbs, face, and torso. Some of the pustules broke out in the mouth and throat, making it almost impossible to breathe or eat.

The Spanish Franciscan friar Motolinia left this description:

"As the Indians did not know the remedy for the disease ... more than half the population died ... They died in heaps, like bedbugs. Many others died of

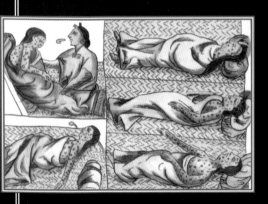

LEFT Smallpox decimated the indigenous population of much of the Americas. The virulent "pox" covered the skin, which peeled off in large deadly slabs.

The proud indigenous inhabitants of Sydney Harbour fell prey to a mysterious disease. It seems likely that the First Fleet brought the contagion.

starvation, because, as they were all taken sick at once, they could not care for each other, nor was there anyone to give them bread or anything else. In many places it happened that everyone in a house died and, as it was impossible to bury the great number of dead, they pulled down the houses over them in order to check the stench that rose from the dead, so that their homes become their tombs."

The pox spread through the population like wildfire. The disease incubates for seven to seventeen days, so people who fled the scourge carried it into new communities. The Mayans dubbed it as *nokakil*, "the great fire." It also traveled quickly along the sophisticated road network built by the Incas.

The diseases penetrated into the heart of North America. When conquistador Hernando de Soto (1486–1542) traveled into the vast interior of the continent, he found large towns and villages abandoned and vacant while vast fields had begun to turn back to nature.

When measles and smallpox combined, indigenous populations were further devastated. This was a trend that followed most European exploration. In the 1870s almost 30 percent of Fijians fell to an outbreak, and the islanders of Samoa, Hawaii, and New Zealand were all similarly affected. Soon after landing at Sydney Cove in 1788, the English settlers noticed that the locals were dying on an unprecedented scale. Each cove, inlet, and cave contained the dead bodies of aborigines who lay unburied as their families had fled in terror.

TURN BACK THE MISSISSIPPI

Hernando de Soto

One more conquistador must be mentioned. Hernando de Soto was one of the first Europeans to penetrate deep into North America.

De Soto had earned a reputation as a brave fighter. In 1532 he put together an expedition to explore the Florida Peninsula. Disease and cruelty had decimated the indigenous slaves working the gold mines in Mexico and Peru and de Soto hoped that the North American mainland might be exploited to offset the shortfall. The Spanish empire was in desperate need of gold as the Italian wars were draining imperial coffers.

In 1539, de Soto sailed from Cuba and disembarked at modern-day Tampa. He then explored what is now Alabama and penetrated deep into the Appalachian Mountains. While traveling through these fertile regions, the Spanish explorers noted that large towns and hundreds of villages had been abandoned, and huge fields lay fallow. European diseases had already made their mark. The expedition reached the Mississippi and here the Spanish found intact civilizations made up of peoples we now know as the mound-builders.

De Soto tried the old conquistador trick of demanding that the chiefs submit to the Spanish as gods newly arrived on Earth. One indigenous leader was wise to de Soto and stated that he would submit if the Spanish could prove their divinity by stopping the flow of the mile-wide Mississippi River. The Spanish bluff was called. The invaders were chased off down the river amid a rain of thousands of javelins and arrows.

De Soto died soon after and the depleted expedition finally found its way back to Tampa. Whispers of the vast new lands soon spread to other European powers.

BELOW In May 1541, de Soto "discovered" the Mississippi River. The locals were not overawed by their visitors and the expedition often had to flee hostile warriors.

The Treaty of Saragossa

With their spectacular success in the Americas and elsewhere, the Spanish and Portuguese decided to expand on the arrangements of the Treaty of Tordesillas (1494). In 1529, the Pope approved the Treaty of Saragossa. This gave all of India and Asia to the two powers. But it could never be enforced. By this time other European powers were looking at exploring new lands and claiming them for themselves.

The First Globe

The first spinning globe ever produced was created by a German, Martin Behaim (1459–1507). Born in Nuremburg, he learned mathematics and astronomy before emigrating to Portugal in 1481. Here Martin joined with some of the greatest brains of the day and set off as the helmsman on a journey in 1484 that got to the Gulf of Guinea and discovered the island of Annobon. They traveled to the mouth of the Congo before returning to Lisbon.

Martin Behaim

The German adventurer then settled in the Azores before making his way back to Nuremberg, where he made the first spinning globe. This showed the Portuguese possessions of the West African Coast.

The globe, which still exists today in the Germanic National Museum of Nuremberg, is the earliest known evidence of the European advance to the Cape of Good Hope and gives an excellent picture of the limits of geographic understanding developed by the best cartographers in the late fifteenth century.

ABOVE Behaim's globe is a remarkable artifact. It not only shows European knowledge of the world, but just as importantly which vast regions were still unexplored.

CHAPTER 4

FOUNDATION OF EMPIRES

THE PORTUGUESE AND THE SPANISH had transformed the world with their ruthless program of exploration, conquest, and colonization. Other European powers looked on with envy. This became a particularly urgent problem when the Portuguese and Spanish crowns were temporarily joined in 1580 under the rule of Philip II (1527–98). But even before this, other nations had embarked on daring schemes of exploration. Powers such as the Dutch, the French, and the English had sent naval expeditions to distant shores—unexplored by Europeans and unexploited. While these seafaring nations explored the oceans, Russian expeditions set off across the vast steppes to the east.

LEFT With Spain and Portugal united under Philip II, most of the known world was ruled by this Most Catholic King.

THE DUTCH, ENGLISH, AND RUSSIANS

Exploration during this period was firmly rooted in commerce. Merchants formed companies that requested "charters," written permission from their monarchs to fund exploratory expeditions to find new lands and new trade items to bring back to Europe. The monarchs granted these companies a monopoly in the areas that were explored. In return, the companies gave the king or queen a percentage of the profits while claiming the lands as part of the monarch's empire. Thus, in European eyes the explorers had a legal right to possess the land and its resources. The indigenous inhabitants were not, of course, consulted.

John Cabot

The first of these royally sponsored explorers was John Cabot (c. 1450–98). Sponsored by King Henry VII (reigned 1485–1509) of England, he set out to find a way to the Pacific Ocean from the Atlantic by traveling through the Arctic. Although Cabot's expedition did not find a northwest passage, he did reach the coast of North America in 1497 at a similar latitude to the Norse discoveries 500 years earlier. This opened up the North American continent for English settlement and found the vast fisheries of cod upon which the new colonies would thrive.

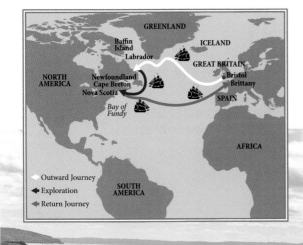

LEFT AND BELOW Cabot's voyage in 1497 was the first known expedition to reach North America since the Vikings. A statue at Bonavista Bay commemorates his first sighting of land at this location.

Sugar and Spice and All Things Nice

Europe's insatiable greed for sugar and spices drove exploration and colonization. Sugar was a valuable commodity and the vast sugar plantations in the Caribbean and Central America demanded a never-ending flow of slaves from Africa.

A range of valuable spices were found in Southeast Asia. Pepper was used as a preservative and to disguise the flavor of rotting meat. Cloves were hugely popular both as a preservative and flavoring agent and as a mild anesthetic. Chewing cloves was also a guarantee against bad breath! Nutmeg, ginger, turmeric, cinnamon, and cardamom were valuable cargoes that originated in India and the Spice Islands of the Molucca Sea (the Maluku Islands in modern-day Indonesia).

By the early seventeeth century the Dutch came to dominate this trade after the creation of the VOC—the Verenigde Oost-Indische Compagnie (Dutch East India Company). This outfit grew so large that it became a rival to nation-states. In 1669, it traded with 150 merchant ships protected by forty men-of-war. It had 50,000 employees and a standing army of 10,000 professional soldiers. By this period, the VOC had taken over many Portuguese trading stations and, from its port of Batavia (Jakarta), monopolized the European spice trade.

The English founded the East India Company, and in the next century armies funded by this corporation explored and conquered much of India.

LEFT **The Dutch East India Company was founded to find valuable spices in the Caribbean and the Americas. Temporary trading stations soon became permanent colonies.**

JACQUES CARTIER

King Francis I of France (reigned 1515–47) was the heir to many decades of conflict with the imperial power of Spain. When Jacques Cartier (1491–1557) approached the throne with a plan to found colonies on the coast of America that would rival Spanish colonies to the south and open up a new trade route through the Northwest Passage, the king jumped at the opportunity. Cartier would lead three expeditions and lay the foundations for the settlement of Canada by the French.

Cartier set out on April 20, 1534. He probably had some experience navigating the waters of the Arctic Circle: The Frenchman was born in St. Malo, a fishing town at the heart of the new cod-fishing industry that was exploiting the vast resources of seafood found by Cabot. It was only a short voyage from those rich mid-Atlantic waters to the shores of North America. Cartier had already studied cartography, mathematics, and astronomy at the French school of navigation at Dieppe—so was well suited to the mission.

ABOVE Jacques Cartier led several exploratory expeditions that laid the foundations for the French colonization of Canada. Despite his great courage, he failed to find gold.

With two ships, Cartier crossed the North Atlantic, successfully navigating the Belle Isle Strait and establishing that Newfoundland was indeed a massive island. He then advanced several miles up the St. Lawrence River before landing on the Gaspé Peninsula. Here he erected a huge 32ft cross as a symbolic claim on the newly discovered land. In September 1534, he returned to St. Malo.

On May 19, 1535, Cartier set off again for the wilds of what we now know as Canada. This mission was not only to scout out the land but also to lay the foundations of a settled country. The plan was to establish new communities, and the explorers also hoped to find large gold reserves. Three ships set out and in September they landed near the St. Lawrence River. The expedition created a village that would later be named Quebec. Twenty-five of Cartier's men died of scurvy in the harsh conditions encountered there. In the spring, the expedition pressed on to another village, which was named Hochelaga—before assuming its modern name of Montreal. Here the explorers came upon the Ottawa River. Cartier's indigenous guides claimed that upstream there were gold deposits that were mined by the local tribes. However, the Frenchmen failed to find any and returned to France disappointed in July 1536. They bore as tribute to the king many valuable pelts but no gold.

ABOVE The vast lands and riches of the New World astounded the European explorers. Here, Cartier discovers the St. Lawrence River in Canada.

On this return journey, Cartier brought aboard their vessels a local chieftain who told the French king that the lands of his peoples were filled with precious metals and spices. The French explorers told a rather less positive tale, however, and it was five years before Francis I would equip another expedition. At least the third expedition knew where they were going. In the Huron and Iroquois language, "*Kanata*" means village and this was corrupted to "Canada" as the name of the new country. On May 23, 1541, a new expedition embarked from the shores of France. It consisted of five ships carrying various individuals including farmers, soldiers, merchants, and even a viceroy of the colony Nouvelle France—"New France."

Cartier's achievements laid the foundations for French colonial expansion. He made one final effort to please his monarch and in 1542 returned for the last time to France bearing gold and diamonds. Sadly for Cartier, on closer investigation his precious cargo proved to be nothing more valuable than copper and loam.

The Iroquois Confederacy

In many parts of North America European explorers came across indigenous peoples who were organized in small tribes that were often at war with their neighbors. This facilitated the rapid conquest of these tribal territories. The Iroquois Confederacy (named after the local longhouses) that explorers encountered in northeast America posed more of a challenge.

The most powerful tribes in the eastern seaboard region formed a powerful confederacy for nearly 200 years—only dissolving at the start of the American Revolutionary War. The fifty top chiefs met in a longhouse, where they coordinated the military actions of their war parties and settled inter-tribal disputes. Tribes included the Mohawk, the Oneida, the Onondaga, the Cayuga, the Seneca, and the Tuscarora.

Explorers and settlers knew that they had to earn the goodwill of the Iroquois if they were to survive in the New World. Their warriors were masters of small-scale warfare and used the dense terrain to perfect the art of ambushing and raiding unwary foes. The Iroquois Confederacy played a large role in the wars between English and French colonial powers in the seventeenth and eighteenth centuries, and for a long time defended their lands from the advancing Europeans.

RIGHT **With the foundation of the Iroquois Confederacy thousands of veteran warriors, skilled in forest warfare, could be launched against indigenous or foreign foes.**

THE DUTCH SETTLEMENT OF NEW YORK

Visitors to New York have to look hard to find traces of the original Dutch settlement at the tip of Manhattan. New Amsterdam was founded in 1625: The foundations of the original city hall can be glimpsed beneath a glassed-in pavement, while some buildings are built in line with the original town plan. Wall Street follows the course of a stockade built to prevent hostile incursions from indigenous neighbors. They, too, have left their mark on the city. Broadway follows an original path used by the Lenape and was adopted by the Dutch as their main thoroughfare. The later grid street plan was overlaid upon this original road. Several explorers were instrumental in the Dutch settlement of the region. The Dutch were determined to seize settlements in the west to balance their possessions in the east.

LEFT AND BELOW The Dutch founded the rich settlement of New Amsterdam, which is now known as New York. Wall Street is delineated by the landward line of fortifications.

Henry Hudson

Both the birth and death of English explorer Henry Hudson (c. 1565–1611) is shrouded in mystery. There is no reference to him until 1607, when he is named in a commission by the Muscovy Trading Company to find the Northwest Passage and a direct route to India. This mission set off from Europe that same year, but was foiled by glaciers. The same thing happened in 1608 and again during another expedition in 1609. There was one major achievement in the third expedition. This was sponsored by the Dutch East India Company and after turning back from the glacial barriers to the north, Hudson sailed past the southern tip of Greenland and reached the coast of North America at Nova Scotia. During this voyage the explorers came across a wide inlet. This was the mouth of the Hudson River—the future location of the city of New York.

ABOVE **Henry Hudson was set adrift by a mutinous crew in the frozen waste of the Arctic Circle. His ultimate fate remains a mystery to this day.**

The pioneering work of Henry Hudson was built upon by Dutch trader Captain Adriaen Block (1567–1627). In four expeditions (1611–14) he explored and mapped the coastline between New Jersey and Massachusetts. He was the first European to enter the Long Island Sound and the Connecticut River, proving that Manhattan was an island and Long Island was a peninsula, both suitable for settlement. Block also established trade with the indigenous inhabitants of Long Island. This facilitated both the purchase of land for the new settlement on Manhattan and the colonization of Connecticut.

Henry Hudson's fate was not to be so happy. On his fourth and last expedition, this time funded by an English cartel, the explorer once again set off in April 1610 to find the Northwest Passage. Some achievements were made during this voyage, including the discovery and naming of the Hudson Strait near Resolution Island. However, in June 1611 Hudson fell to that perennial danger of many early explorers when his crew mutinied against their commander. Hudson, his son, and seven loyal seamen were put in a sloop and told to find their own way home.

They never did. None of the forlorn party was ever seen again and only a few of the original crew returned to England where they were punished for mutiny. They did, however, bring Hudson's charts, which were of immeasurable assistance to later expeditions.

NAVIGATION IN THE AGE OF EXPLORATION

DURING THE RENAISSANCE of the fourteenth to seventeenth centuries, the understanding of longitude and latitude was formalized, and mapmaking became much more sophisticated.

Latitude and Longitude

To determine a ship's latitude, navigators measured the height of stars or the sun in the sky. As they moved closer to the equator, the north star would be nearer the horizon. The astrolabe was a vital piece of kit. This round brass instrument used two plates on a rotating arm to measure the angle between a celestial body such as the sun and the "zenith," the point directly above the ship. The astrolabe was best used on land or in calm seas as readings could be distorted in rough conditions.

The quadrant was a wedge-shaped device with a plumb line hanging from the top corner. It would be lined up with the sun, and the point at which the plumb line crossed the curved bottom of the wedge would give a reading of its height in degrees.

Finding the longitude of a vessel was much more difficult and relied on dead reckoning—as during the Viking age. This process involved an estimate of how far the ship had traveled from east to west or vice versa. An experienced navigator could accurately predict the rate of movement, but did have some basic devices to assist them. Sand glasses would be used to measure time and this would be compared with a rope thrown behind a moving ship. The rope had a piece of timber tied at the end that caused it to unravel behind the ship. Along the rope knots were tied at intervals of about 50ft. Sailors counted the number of knots released and compared this with the amount of time revealed by the sand glasses—thus estimating the "rate of knots" at which the ship was sailing.

The riddle of fixing longitude was not solved until John Harrison (1693–1776) invented the chronometer in 1735, so winning a £20,000 prize from the British government's Board of Longitude.

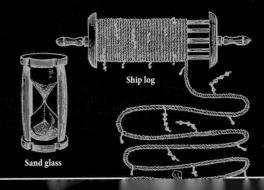

Ship log

Sand glass

Chronometer

Cartographers and Spies

During this period, cartographers came into their own. Using data and charts brought home by seafarers, they were able to create accurate "portolan charts." These maps were sophisticated navigational aids that detailed the distance between ports or harbors—hence the name. Hazards and dangers, as well as details of the best times to sail, were included on the charts. Horizontal lines depicting latitude and vertical lines showing longitude became a feature of the maps in the sixteenth century.

Another aid to navigation were "roteiros." These contained detailed information on currents and landmarks that ensured the seafarers were heading in the right direction. Such charts were zealously guarded by the different empires that produced them. Much blood, sweat, and tears were expended in discovering these lucrative trade routes, and they were of course reluctant to share the valuable information with rival trading powers.

RIGHT *Travel Account of the Voyage of the Sailor Jan Huyghen van Linschoten to the Portuguese East India.*

One of the first great acts of commercial espionage was conducted by the adventurous Dutchman Jan Huyghen van Linshoten (1563–1611). Traveling to Spain and Portugal, he obtained a position with the Archbishop of Goa's household and soon proceeded to this thriving port on the coast of India. Goa was the jewel in the crown of Portuguese possessions and the hub of their extensive trade networks throughout the Spice Islands of the East. For five years the Dutchman lived in this colony, gathering data and information on trade networks throughout Asia.

When van Linshoten returned home, he wrote the *Itinerario,* which included charts showing how to get there. Published in 1596, the book was a best seller and the newly formed Dutch East India Company (VOC) used the information contained therein to wrest control of many colonies from the weakened Portuguese.

Sir Francis Drake

The swashbuckling Francis Drake (c. 1540–96) was England's foremost explorer. Not only did he play merry havoc with Spanish shipping in the Spanish Main (the Gulf of Mexico) and defeat the Spanish Armada (1588), he was the second mariner to circumnavigate the Earth (in 1577–80).

In 1573 Drake was embarked upon an expedition not usually associated with exploration. With 100 men he had set an ambush in the heart of the densely wooded Spanish Main. In March 1573, the future admiral teamed up with some disreputable French pirates and freed African slaves in order to carry out one of the greatest thefts of the decade. Along the path came a convoy of mules, heavily laden with booty stripped from the mines of Peru, on their way to port for shipping to Madrid.

Drake and his men descended on the mule train, disarmed the Spanish guard and found themselves the proud possessors of around fifteen tons of gold and silver. His fortune was made. But that was not all. On this expedition, Drake was the first Englishman to glimpse the Pacific.

Drake continued his depredations. Sailing in two fast "privateers," he became a scourge of Spanish shipping along the Atlantic coast. With a "letter of marque" from Queen Elizabeth I (reigned 1558–1603), he created such chaos that the Spaniards

RIGHT AND BELOW **Francis Drake burst onto the world scene and was quick to challenge Spanish supremacy of the seas while circumnavigating the world. He was the first Englishman to see the Pacific Ocean.**

dubbed him El Draque ("The Dragon"). The Englishman was condemned as a pirate, and Spanish emperor Philip II put a bounty of 20,000 ducats on his head. The Spaniards soon became convinced that Drake had supernatural powers. El Draque, they said, had done a deal with the devil and got his crooked hands on a magic mirror that revealed the location of every Spanish ship and showed what bounty she carried.

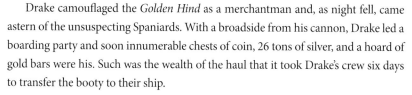

Sir Francis Drake

Drake's real talent was superb seamanship. This was clearly shown on his greatest coup of all—the capture in March 1579 of the Spanish treasure ship, the *Nuestra Señora de la Concepción* ("Our Lady of the Immaculate Conception"). Hearing of the vast riches about to be shipped back to Spain, Drake and his vessel the *Golden Hind* slipped into the Pacific through the Strait of Magellan and made their way northward to where their quarry lay. Sighting the *Concepción* while at full sail, Drake did not want to alarm it by approaching too fast. If he reduced sail, the Spaniards would become suspicious. Drake had several laden barrels thrown over the stern. They caused a drag, slowing his ship without alerting the Spaniards to the speed of his craft.

Drake camouflaged the *Golden Hind* as a merchantman and, as night fell, came astern of the unsuspecting Spaniards. With a broadside from his cannon, Drake led a boarding party and soon innumerable chests of coin, 26 tons of silver, and a hoard of gold bars were his. Such was the wealth of the haul that it took Drake's crew six days to transfer the booty to their ship.

Drake's story was one of rags to riches. Born to a poor family in Devon, he was bundled off to serve in a coastal shipper at the age of twelve. In 1565, he joined his cousin on a slave ship convoy heading to Mexico, and in the port of Rio de la Hacha, they were attacked by Spaniards who sank two of their three ships. Further run-ins with Spaniards cemented Drake's hatred of the country and its people.

On November 15, 1577, now captain, Drake set out on his most ambitious journey of all. The dashing privateer was at the head of five ships: the *Golden Hind*, the *Elizabeth*, the *Swan*, the *Marygold*, and the *Christoph*. He set off with a commission from Queen Elizabeth I to advance into the "South Seas" and compete with the Spanish by founding new colonies. The first stop was the Cape Verde Islands, where they took on supplies. From here the fleet sailed through the South Atlantic and along the coastlines of Brazil and Argentina. After progressing through the Strait of Magellan, he made several important discoveries while exploring the frigid waters of the south. He proved that Tierra del Fuego was not part of a great southern continent, and discovered the Drake Passage that separates this southern tip of South America and Antarctica.

BELOW **In April 1581, Queen Elizabeth visited Drake on his legendary vessel the *Golden Hind*. She bestowed many honors on the daring mariner, including a knighthood.**

Turning northward, he plundered his way along the Peruvian coast. Near Cape San Francisco, the *Golden Hind* carried out the coup against the *Nuestra Señora de la Concepción*. Piracy was one thing, but to fulfill his remit Drake also had to seize some land for his queen. He continued north in an effort to find a northwest passage then turned back and claimed land around present-day San Francisco as "Nova Albion."

In July 1579, Drake set off across the vast reaches of the Pacific. He reached Timor, proved that Java was an island, before rounding the Cape of Good Hope, and returning to Plymouth on September 26, 1580. He was greeted as a national hero: the plunder he had stripped from the Spanish exceeded the English crown's yearly revenue.

Drake was knighted by Queen Elizabeth and made a commander of the fledgling British navy. However, such slights to the Spanish crown could not go unanswered, and King Philip II of Spain began to assemble an armada to invade England in retaliation in 1586. Drake proved his mastery of European waters and disrupted the Spanish preparation with sustained attacks on Cadiz and Lisbon. He also maintained an extensive spy network in Spanish ports and was able to ascertain every move the Spaniards would make when they invaded in 1588. The armada was defeated, thanks in part to Drake's superior seamanship.

Eventually Drake died of dysentery at sea off Puerto Bello (modern Panama). As befitting a gallant buccaneer, his body was clad in full armor, sealed in a lead coffin, and consigned to the deep.

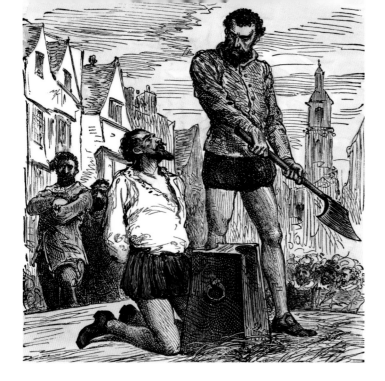

RIGHT Sir Walter Raleigh was not so lucky. Not only did he fail to find El Dorado, but an agreement with the Spanish saw the explorer losing his head.

Sir Walter Raleigh

Another explorer who enjoyed the favor of Queen Elizabeth I was Sir Walter Raleigh (c. 1554–1618), who was sponsored in 1584 to explore any uncharted and uncolonized regions in the Americas. He would get a share of any gold mined there and was also expected to act as a privateer, seizing Spanish shipping. Raleigh led several successful expeditions. In 1585, he sponsored the first English colony in America on Roanoke Island. In 1587, Raleigh explored the region from North Carolina to Florida and named the newly found territories Virginia in honor of the "Virgin Queen," one of the titles of the unmarried Elizabeth I. He made two expeditions to find El Dorado and in 1595 discovered modern-day French Guiana. Sadly for Raleigh, he fell out of royal favor once Elizabeth I died, being charged with treason for plotting against her successor James I (reigned 1603–25). He was executed in Westminster on October 29, 1618.

Sir Walter Raleigh

While Roanoke was not a permanent settlement and failed within five years, Drake did make several permanent contributions to English life from the New World. He popularized the potato in England as well as the use of tobacco. He left a tobacco pouch in his cell that said *Comes meus fuit in illo miserrimo tempore* ("It was my companion at that most miserable time").

Headhunters on Borneo

European explorers soon learned that there were places that yielded little profit and were full of unspeakable dangers. One of the most feared foreign locations was the island of Borneo. The waters around the island were infested with fierce pirate bands. Fugitive Chinese, fierce Malays, and the Sea Dayak would head out from well-defended inlets and seize any passing shipping. Few survived these encounters and any Europeans who fell into the hands of these desperadoes were guaranteed a painful and prolonged death.

ABOVE **Many Europeans suffered a grisly fate when exploring the wilds of Borneo. Here a luckless explorer is seized by Dayaks.**

The coast of this vast island was dangerous enough, but the jungle-covered interior held even greater terrors. The indigenous tribes excelled at headhunting. Before an Iban male could marry, he had to raid a neighboring tribe and bring back a head. The warrior was then filled with the spirit of his victim. If he succeeded in this deadly rite of passage, squiggly lines would be tattooed on the back of his hands.

The Murut tribe was particularly feared. Anybody could be a victim—children, women, and the aged—all were fair game. Any young man who failed in this quest was ostracized and shamed by his family and tribe. The Kadazan-Dusun restricted themselves to the heads of neighboring warriors, but there was one caveat: The victim could only be beheaded while he was alive. Otherwise the spirit would flee before it could be taken by the victorious warrior.

To fall into the hands of the Sea Dayaks, who ventured out in their huge war canoes, was a terrible fate. They would chop off a head before using a range of implements to extract the brain through the nasal cavity or with a spoon from the base of the neck. The head was then smoked over a fire: Warriors did not hesitate to come and slice off a piece of flesh for a snack!

Few Europeans explored the center of Borneo. It became a semi-autonomous colony under the British adventurer James Brooke as "the White Raja" in 1842. He made some progress in eliminating the practice of head hunting, although it made something of a resurgence under Japanese rule in World War II.

ABOVE **As the first European to meet with the cannibalistic Bytak tribe, Ida Pfeiffer said that she was "too old and tough to make good eating."**

Austria never founded an overseas empire, but they did have one famous explorer who visited much of the known, and unknown, world. Ida Pfeiffer (1797–1858) made several trips around the world and spent months living in Madagascar and more than a year living among the tribes of Borneo, including cannibal tribes. Like many other explorers she succumbed to a disease picked up during her travels—most likely Malaria.

Exploring Siberia

Three Russian explorers were key to the European exploration of Siberia: Yermak Timofeyevich (c. 1532–85), Yerofey Pavlovich Khabarov (1603–71), and Vitus Bering (1681–1741).

Yermak Timofeyevich

In the sixteenth century Siberia was one of the last great frontiers for European explorers. It was a place of mystery and danger. Even in the twenty-first century, this wild and hostile environment is still giving up long-held secrets.

Hundreds of thousands of years ago, a mysterious race of proto-humans moved into the barren wastes of Siberia. Now known as the Denisovans (from a cave that revealed the original artifacts of these people), they thrived until modern humans moved through their territories. Just as these early human explorers and settlers interbred with the Neanderthals, so modern *Homo sapiens* interbred with the Denisovans, picking up some of their DNA in the process. Some Asian populations have some Denisovan DNA and it is believed that the modern-day inhabitants of Tibet and Nepal, which includes the Sherpa, can exist in an oxygen-poor environment at high altitudes thanks to this inheritance.

BELOW **Waterways were often used to penetrate into the wilds of Siberia. Cossack explorers used their superior weapons to subdue the indigenous inhabitants.**

For hundreds of years, the Russian states had groaned under the rule of the Mongol khans. But by the time Ivan ascended to the throne of Russia in 1547 the "Tatars," as they were known, were more of a nuisance than a real threat. Ivan created one of the first centralized European states and after defeating the nomadic horsemen in battle decided to expand to the east. Up until then the Russian state had not expanded beyond the Ural Mountains. This dangerous frontier had swallowed up many an expedition, but when a band of Cossacks 700 strong set off in 1579 to cross the barrier and exploit its resources an eastward expansion that would last for hundreds of years began.

Yermak
Timofeyevich

Cossacks were a wild, freewheeling group of hardy horsemen who lived in large bands around the Don and Volga rivers. Many were escaped serfs who resented any authority, and one of their leaders was Yermak Timofeyevich, who had gained a reputation for piracy. He was commissioned to lead an expedition across the Urals to subdue the wild peoples living there.

Once the band had crossed the Urals, they built boats and sped swiftly along the River Tobol. Tatars sought to stop the Cossacks, but modern firearms gave the explorers the edge and soon they penetrated as far as Sibir, the nomad horsemen's capital. Here they settled in for the winter, gathering food from the locals, who initially welcomed the explorers. In spring of 1580, the expedition traveled along the River Ob—a major waterway that empties into the Arctic Ocean.

By 1581, Yermak's men were unwilling to continue. Many had died in fierce battles with the local tribes or else perished in the freezing Siberian conditions, which in some places were colder than those at the North Pole. Yermak took a gamble and dispatched a trusted follower with 5,000 valuable pelts from exotic arctic animals such as beavers, foxes, and bears to the court of Ivan the Terrible in an effort to get more money and men from the emperor. The cargo reached Moscow in 1582 and tempted the emperor to invest in further expansion. For two more years Yermak continued his march into Siberia, mapping rivers and resources as he went. A gift from the tsar proved to be the Cossack explorer's undoing. In August 1584, his party was ambushed while traveling along the Irtysh River. Yermak jumped out of the boat to escape wearing a mail coat provided by Ivan—and sank to his death.

Yerofey Pavlovich Khabarov

For several decades after Yermak's death there were no organized expeditions to Siberia. Freebooters, trappers, and hunters continued to pour into the region, but no claims were made by the central government in Moscow.

Yerofey Pavlovich Khabarov brought much of Siberia under the control of the tsars. By exploring and then conquering the Amur River region in southeastern Siberia, he made Russia the largest empire in the world. The Amur River became the border between two great states of Manchu China and Romanov Russia. Khabarov was born 450 miles north of Moscow and led several successful trading missions into the frozen wilds around Finland and the Arctic Circle. He then turned toward Siberia and passed through Yakutsk, the easternmost European settlement on Siberia's Lena River. This wild and rough outpost was used by fur trappers to deliver their goods and grab supplies before heading back out into the wilderness. In the mid-1640s a group of these trappers returned from the wilds and told of a rich area filled with game and gold. They dubbed the region Daurien and the river on which it was located was called the Amur.

BELOW **Many of the Russian explorers have monuments to their achievements. Here Yerofey Pavlovich Khabarov gazes over the town founded in his honor.**

Khabarov had already made a fortune by establishing a salt mine at Yakutsk and he was keen to explore the new region. He requested permission from the tsar's regional administrator, the *voivode*, to lead an expedition. To get royal assent to the proposal would have taken months, so with a sleight of hand the official issued Khabarov arms and commissioned him to carry out an expedition to the Amur River in the name of the tsar. The *voivode* agreed to split the loot, sending notice to Moscow *after* the expedition set off. Over the next two years Khabarov, and his men mapped the rich region. They imposed a reign of terror on the local peoples—plundering stores of food, burning villages, and indiscriminately butchering women and children.

He and other explorers had other allies—smallpox and influenza. Before European penetration of their domains, the indigenous inhabitants were dispersed over vast areas. It is estimated that by 1709 there were perhaps a quarter of a million people living in a region encompassing 5 million square miles. Vast distances and cold weather made transmission of bacteria and microbes almost impossible. But when the new arrivals came, they brought diseases to which the locals had no resistance. Perhaps 80 percent of the indigenous population died from these illnesses.

In 1652, Khabarov's good fortune came to an end. Hearing of the violence on the frontier, the Manchu sent an army to stop the Cossacks and forced the Russians to withdraw from the border. In 1653, a detachment of the Russian army turned up. The explorer was arrested and hauled across the steppes all the way to Moscow. He was put on trial, his assets were seized, and he faced execution. However, despite the cruelty Khabarov had shown to his men and the indigenous tribes, his tales of riches and glory rehabilitated him in the eyes of the tsar. The explorer had his reputation and wealth restored and he gained the official role of governor of southern Siberia. The town of Khabarovsk on the Amur River was founded in his honor.

Vitus Bering

The third great explorer of Russia was Vitus Bering. When Peter I "the Great" (1672–1725) ascended the throne in 1682, the Russian empire was growing fat on the vast wealth coming out of Siberia. Most of the hostile tribes had been subdued in the first half of the century, but there were still many mysteries to be solved. Was Asia joined by a land bridge to north America? How long was the coastline of the Arctic Ocean?

In 1725, Bering's expedition set out from St. Petersburg and traveled through Siberia until it reached the Pacific Ocean. Here the adventurers built a small fleet and sailed to the Kamchatka Peninsula. Sailing north west, Bering traversed what is now known as the Bering Strait separating Alaska from Siberia. The expedition returned, mapping the coast of the Arctic Ocean all the way to Archangel in 1730.

Another expedition followed in the early 1740s. The Great Northern Expedition reached Alaska, which was claimed as a Russian possession (and would be sold to the United States in 1867). The expedition also mapped the Aleutian Islands.

Although a stunning success, this adventure ended badly. Scurvy and foul weather took a deadly toll, and many died. Bering and his party were marooned on the Commander Islands, where frostbite laid them low. The Arctic foxes that roamed on the island were not afraid of humans and often had to be fought off. Bering perished, but a small group of his men survived and—using wreckage from their boat—built a raft with which they managed to return to Kamchatka and tell of Bering's fate.

Strange Creatures

Explorers often came upon strange and mysterious beasts. Even as empires were established that covered the globe, some areas of mystery remained.

Colonel Percy Fawcett (1867–c. 1925) was one of the last great English eccentrics. After a career in the military, he developed an obsessional belief that the remains of a great lost city, which he called "Z," was to be found in the heart of the Amazonian jungle. This was despite the fact that in the sixteenth and seventeenth centuries countless expeditions had penetrated deep into the Amazon in pursuance of this quest. He believed he would find the remains of a mighty civilization that had thrived there in prehistory and developed its own hieroglyphic writing. Between 1906 and 1925, Fawcett made many expeditions in pursuit of the ruins. He became friends with the authors H. Rider Haggard and Arthur Conan Doyle, who used many of the explorer's tales in their own books.

Fawcett disappeared during his last expedition in 1925. How he died is still a mystery—many suspect he ended up in the bellies of one of the many Amazonian tribes.

Before he disappeared, the colonel described many strange animals. These included a 62ft-long giant anaconda and a huge man-eating spider. No doubt the most amazing critters he and his companions encountered were the Maricoxi—legendary man-beasts living in the heart of the Amazonian jungle. While his reports may be considered tall tales, they were corroborated by many of his fellow explorers.

In 1914 he and his party had penetrated deep into the uncharted region called the Matto Grosso. Local tribes in what we now know as Bolivia spoke of some hairy upright creatures that had wonderful skills at hunting and liked nothing more than eating the flesh of humans. While traveling through the jungle, the party encountered a new tribe of humans who called themselves the Maxubis. Although they appeared to be primitive hunter-gatherers, the Maxubis were able to demonstrate a remarkable knowledge of the movement of planets and the sun.

Penetrating deeper into the jungle, the explorers found a path used by remarkably hairy individuals with very

Bird-eating tarantula

long arms, sloping foreheads, and rigid, protruding eyebrows. These strange creatures were carrying primitive bows and arrows and disappeared into the jungle when spotted by the Europeans. For the next few nights unearthly horn-like sounds echoed around the traveling party and Fawcett and his men had no doubt that the strange beings were shadowing their every move. The men stumbled upon a primitive camp filled with rude shelters dug into the ground and were suddenly surrounded by the hostile hominids. The village's inhabitants drew their primitive but sharp arrows and surrounded Fawcett and his men. The colonel drew an old Mauser pistol and discharged it into the ground. In the blink of an eye the Maricoxi, as the locals called these hominids, fled into the jungle, but not before they had loosed several arrows at the intruders.

The Europeans decided not to pursue and over the next few days left the territory of the strange hairy apemen.

Explorers have often reported strange creatures. English Victorian explorers Henry Morton Stanley (1841–1904) and David Livingstone (1813–73) reported seeing strange striped donkey-like animals in the Congo in the late 1880s. Their description of the mysterious animal as the "African unicorn" was

Anaconda

greeted with skepticism, but in 1901 a specimen was found and the animal is now recognized as the okapi—a distant relative of the giraffe.

In 1776 a French explorer heard reports of a huge long-necked animal living in the wettest areas of the Congo. Now known as the Mokele-mbembe, the strange creature is Africa's version of the Loch Ness Monster. Even now European explorers penetrate deep into the Congo wetlands in an attempt to track down the elusive animal.

CHAPTER 5

THE PACIFIC

THE PACIFIC COVERS more than 30 percent of
the Earth's surface—60 million square miles.
While the Northern Pacific has an occasional
archipelago, such as the Aleutian Islands, most
of the island landforms are in the Southern Pacific.
They are divided into three regions: Melanesia covers
the regions around Papua New Guinea and stretches
out eastward to Fiji. North of this is Micronesia,
scattered islands tucked into the side of Southeast
Asia that include the Mariana and Marshall island
chains. Lastly, is Polynesia, one of the last frontiers
to be settled by humans. Its three points rest roughly
on Hawaii, New Zealand, and Easter Island.

LEFT **Two very different worlds
collided when explorers such as
Captain Cook encountered the
diverse cultures of the Pacific,
exemplified by this heavily
tattooed Maori chieftain.**

HUMAN EXPLORATION AND SETTLEMENT OF THE ASIA PACIFIC

Peking Man

When Europeans finally ventured into the Pacific they "discovered" a wonderland of unique cultures adapted to live off the bounty that the ocean provided. Living on island paradises and in harmony with the environment, the peoples of the great ocean enchanted the explorers who braved the vast distances of the Pacific.

These were no isolated peoples, living apart from any other culture, cut off by water—it appears that they knew of communities thousands of miles away and regularly visited them. Just as the ancient Greeks called the Mediterranean a Greek lake, so the indigenous inhabitants of the Pacific treated it as their own lake that was crisscrossed by generation after generation.

The story of the human exploration and settlement of the Asia-Pacific region was once thought to be simple. As recently as 2000, conventional wisdom painted a linear progression of events. Approximately 1 million years ago *Homo erectus* emerged out of Africa, moved through the Eurasian continent, and explored and settled over hundreds of thousands of years, before ending up in Java. Fossils such as Peking Man and Java Man support this idea. *Homo erectus* was physically very similar to modern humans, but lacked a large brain or sophisticated vocal communications.

Then, according to this scenario, about 80,000 or 70,000 years ago, modern humans moved out of their African homeland and destroyed all hominids who lay in their path. The Neanderthals of Europe were quickly replaced and within 20,000 years all other hominids, including *Homo erectus*, were wiped out by the advancing moderns. By about 50,000 BCE these humans—*Homo sapiens*—had made a last leap over deep water and colonized Papua New Guinea and Australia. At this time, the land masses were connected into a super-continent now known as Sahul. This narrative was, except for a few anomalies, borne out in the fossil record.

All very neat and simple. All very wrong.

BELOW **The conventional view of our origins saw hominid evolution progressing in clear stages. A much more complex picture has recently emerged.**

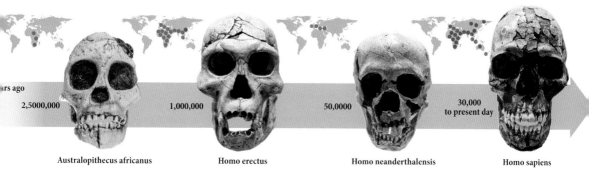

rs ago

2,5000,000 — *Australopithecus africanus*

1,000,000 — *Homo erectus*

50,0000 — *Homo neanderthalensis*

30,000 to present day — *Homo sapiens*

The first chink in the armor of this theory came about when a remarkable archeological discovery was made on the Indonesian island of Flores in 2004. *Homo floresiensis* (nicknamed "the Hobbit" after the short-statured race imagined by British writer J. R. R. Tolkein [1892–1973]) was a tiny primitive human who stood about 3ft tall. S/he used fire and stone tools and may have survived as recently as 16,000 years ago, coexisting with modern human settlers. Many scientists refused to acknowledge that it was a new species and insisted that the creatures were in fact deformed or diseased humans. *Homo floresiensis* did not fit in the accepted timeline. Since then, a close study of their wrist bones has indicated that they were an offshoot of *Homo erectus*.

Recent DNA studies have also indicated that the humans who moved through Eurasia did not eliminate the Neanderthals but instead interbred with them. Modern Europeans and Asians have approximately 2 percent of Neanderthal DNA. A stunning discovery in a cave in Siberia revealed a new ancestor. A finger bone from a young female was found in the Denisova Cave in the Altai Mountains in Siberia in 2010. DNA testing found that this new line of peoples, the Denisovans, were genetically distinct from modern humans and Neanderthals. They ranged from Siberia all through Southeast Asia and all the way to the Pacific. Melanesians, Papuans, and Aboriginal Australians have significant elements of Denisovan DNA. It also seems that Neanderthals mated with Denisovans and the hybrids mated with modern

Homo sapien

Homo Floresiensis

RIGHT AND BELOW **Over hundreds of thousands of years, myriad different hominid species evolved in many different environments. All of these dates are approximate only.**

Modern humans left Africa interbred with Neanderthals in the middle east around 60,000 years ago and with Denisovans before 45,000 years ago.

Range
■ Neanderthal
■ Homo Erectus

Route out of Afica
Homo Sapien
in Africa 200,000 years ago

Denisovans 2010
40,000 years ago

40,000   25,000   15,000

Jinniushan Man 1984
200,000 years ago

200,000   70,000

Dali Man 1978
200,000 years ago

30,000

200,000

50,000

1200

Homo Floresiensis 2004
94,000-13,000 years ago

humans. In addition, studies have revealed that the Papuans and Australians interbred with two more races of archaic humans who were living in the Sahul region before the modern humans arrived. These races are only known by the remnant DNA found in existing peoples. They are to all intents "shadow" races only known through traces of DNA.

After about 50,000 BCE, the inhabitants of Sahul continued exploring eastward. They occupied the Bismarck archipelago and reached as far as the Solomon Islands—what is now termed near-Oceania or Melanesia. No known explorations took place beyond these points into the distant islands of Polynesia. Perhaps rising sea levels made the prospect of penetrating into the heart of the Pacific too daunting. The only other human impact on the Pacific during this time was the settlement of the Pacific coast by Amerindians moving down the coast after they crossed the Bering Strait from Asia approximately 13,000 years ago.

Around 4,000 years ago, prehistory's last great pulse of exploration began. Out of the western Pacific emerged a new seagoing culture that left the security of island chains behind. Polynesian migrations erupted out of Southeast Asia in approximately 2000 BCE and reached the Solomon and Fijian islands in this initial phase. Most Polynesians carry DNA known as the "Polynesian motif," which suggests they originated in Indonesia and the Philippines. Samoa was reached by 1000 BCE and the final drives for exploration and settlement saw the Hawaiian Islands settled by 400 CE, the Cook Islands by 600 CE, and New Zealand by the Maori in approximately 1200 CE.

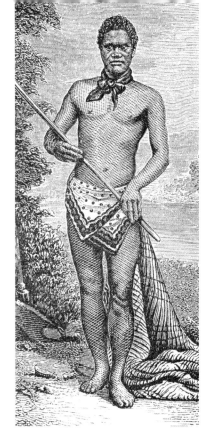

ABOVE **The Maoris represented the last phase of human migration when they colonized New Zealand in approximately 1200 CE. The islands were a Garden of Eden.**

The ancestors of the modern-day inhabitants of Polynesia made these tremendous voyages in twin-hulled canoes. They carried a living larder such as pigs, chickens, and root vegetables. Less-welcome guests accompanied these explorers—the Pacific rat devastated many ecosystems. Explorers such as Captain James Cook (1728–79) of England found peoples whose entire way of life was orientated to moving across the vast ocean of the Pacific and utilizing its resources. They all had a language with a common root and shared stories of an original homeland.

Debates about the extent of the land the Polynesians settled on abound. Recent findings have debunked an earlier theory that suggested some fourteenth-century chicken bones found in Chile proved that the Polynesians had reached its shores, but there is still some uncertainty on this matter.

EUROPEANS REACH THE HEART OF POLYNESIA

Álvaro de Mendaña

For many years Europeans had played along the edges of the Pacific. The American coasts were gradually explored and colonized by the new imperial powers—as was Southeast Asia. However, apart from a couple of quick dashes through the ocean while circumnavigating the world, no real exploration of the islands of Polynesia took place until the seventeenth century.

The Marquesas

Spanish explorer Álvaro de Mendaña (1542–95) was the first European to discover a Pacific island community on the Marquesas in the central Pacific. This contact between cultures would echo many later encounters.

In 1567–69 Mendaña had traveled from Lima in Peru in two ships to find the "Great Southern Land." For hundreds of years rumors of a huge landmass, situated in the southern hemisphere to balance the landmasses in the northern hemisphere, had inspired explorers.

Sponsored by King Philip II—who was convinced the missing continent would be home to the legendary gold mines of the biblical King Solomon—the expedition set out across the Pacific. After sailing for more than 6,000 miles, they came upon a large landmass on February 7, 1568. At first Mendaña was convinced that this was the goal of his journey, but with further exploration it became clear that it was a large island that was part of an extensive archipelago—now named the Solomons. For six months the Spaniards explored the region.

Initially, the relations between the indigenous inhabitants and their visitors were cordial, but when Mendaña was offered the severed arm and shoulder of a child as a meal he decided to move on. Penetrating into Micronesia the expedition noted the Marshall Islands and then Wake Island, before returning to the Californian coast and thence back to Lima.

Years later, in 1595, on a journey to establish a colony on the Solomon Islands, Mendaña stumbled upon the Marquesas five weeks after setting out from Peru. As he approached the southernmost island, now known as Fatu Hiva, seventy canoes pulled out to welcome the visitors. The Spanish explorers seemed to have entered some kind of paradise. The canoes were laden with foods such as coconuts and plantains. Their occupants offered sealed sections of bamboo pipe filled with fresh water. Even though they were heavily laden with people, the canoes sped across the waters of the bay and were remarkably stable. They had outriggers off the main hull, the invention that allowed exploration of Oceania by the early pioneers. Hundreds of other people swam around the Spanish ships, climbing on or off canoes as the fancy took them.

The inhabitants were without fear, a common feature of first encounters. Rather than viewing the strange visitors as aliens or gods, they saw them merely as travelers with bigger boats than usual. The Marquesans climbed aboard the ships, where they touched the soldiers' arms and accoutrements without a trace of fear.

The visitors were struck by the beauty of the indigenous peoples. The men and women were perfectly proportioned with shapely limbs, long fingers, beautiful eyes, and perfect teeth. Most were naked and wearing their hair long "like women"—their only dress seemed to be a blue paint. This was of course extensive tattooing, a common practice throughout the Pacific, and in fact, the name is derived from the Polynesian word *tatau*. The inhabitants of the Marquesas perfected this art and every inch of the body could be decorated, including the eyelids, the palms of their hands, and even their tongues.

Over two weeks, Mendaña's expedition explored the archipelago. They found a land of plenty, with the inhabitants feasting on a huge array of seafood as well as pigs, chickens, plantains, coconuts, and breadfruit. Such was the abundance that large amounts of food were offered to wooden idols residing in circular enclosures.

What most impressed the explorers was the array of canoes. Some were fitted out to carry one or two people, while other heavily built vessels could carry up to forty people for what must have been long distances. The distances can only be guessed at, but the *Te Enata* ("the People"), as they referred to themselves, told the Spaniards of numberless islands to be found over the horizon. In one remarkable incident, a darker-skinned man was noticed on one of the Spanish ships. The *Te Enata* gestured toward the horizon and told of another people who resembled the sailor and used bows and arrows. This weapon was not used in Polynesia—which continent could they be referring to?

Once Mendaña left the islands on his doomed attempt to settle the Solomon Islands, the *Te Enata* would be left to their own devices for almost 200 years. They would have been glad to see him go— the Spaniards had killed several hundred of the inhabitants during their brief sojourn.

RIGHT European explorers noticed that the inhabitants of Polynesia shared many cultural similarities. Housing styles, tools, and languages were obvious signs that they were related.

POLYNESIANS—
AT ONE WITH THE OCEAN

URING THE 4,000 YEARS that the Polynesians settled the vast southern Pacific they developed an intimate knowledge of the ocean and its ways. They also developed an impressive toolkit that allowed them to utilize its resources and navigate the vast distances involved.

Their technology revolved around fishing. The reefs and atolls of the Pacific are some of the richest environments on Earth. Fish, shellfish, turtles, octopuses, and crustaceans abounded in the shallow waters, while deep-sea fish such as tuna and dolphin were also their prey. They created perfectly designed nets and hooks for each type of animal, as well as fish

traps that took advantage of tidal flows: hooks made from turtle shell or oysters acted like lures and their flashing surfaces attracted fish from afar. Their spears were viciously barbed with sharks' teeth or jagged pieces of shell. Despite this impressive array of fishing equipment, the Polynesians were careful not to exhaust fishing stocks and only caught some fish one or two weeks of the year.

Polynesians developed an extensive vocabulary suited to their environment and their intimate knowledge of tides and seawater was reflected in their vocabulary. They had words to distinguish between different types of pool, passage, beach, and isthmus. Different words for breakers, foam, swells, and waves presented precise and valuable information to the listener. Water that was "alive" was open while "dead" water was restricted by bays or atolls. A knowledge of the characteristics of reefs and coral could often mean the difference between life and death.

LEFT Polynesians exploited the rich marine environment using materials found on the islands they inhabited. Clothing was made from natural fibers, and sometimes, furs.

One word that the Polynesians used that has no English equivalent is the term * katae*, the side of the canoe without a supporting outrigger—the free side. English explorer Captain James Cook noted the vast array of canoes during his travels in Polynesia. Small fishing vessels would have a simple outrigger made with a sharpened length of bamboo, while royal vessels belonging to great chiefs would be as long as European ships and have a beautifully carved and ornate outrigger. Deeper vessels could carry cargo, and some had decks built between the canoe and its stabilizer. These were used for long-distance trading or exploratory missions. Cook noted that Tahitian kings built large catamaran-like vessels with two hulls. The indigenous people built canoes on an almost industrial scale, using the simplest of tools. When not in use these precious vessels were hauled onshore and sheltered in huge woven reed hangers.

Perhaps the most impressive seafarers were the inhabitants of the Tuamotu Archipelago. Stretching for 800 miles across the Pacific, this is the largest chain of atolls on Earth. Atolls, or "low islands," are coral formations rarely rising above 20ft. While rich in sea life, they lack freshwater or large trees. Early explorers of the archipelago noted that the indigenous peoples wandered over the islands like nomads, taking resources and moving on when new foods were needed.

ABOVE A range of outrigger canoes could be used for short fishing trips or for more ambitious oceanic journeys. The Polynesians eventually lost this skill.

The inhabitants were the supreme boat-builders of the region. They did not have large trees, so made use of any piece of timber or driftwood. They would tie pieces together with twine and ropes before waterproofing with elaborate combinations of carved tortoise shells.

Polynesians did not have the words to categorize the vast distances. Instead these experienced navigators described far-off places by the number of days it took to sail there. Tupaia (c. 1725–1770) from Tahiti, who accompanied James Cook on much of his first voyage in 1768–71, could predict to the hour when an island would be sighted. Even the depths of inlets and coves were no mystery. This remarkable man produced a map that showed the location of up to seventy islands stretching across 2,000 miles of Pacific Ocean.

TASMANIA, NEW ZEALAND, TONGA, AND FIJI

Abel Tasman

When Dutch explorer Abel Tasman (1603–59) first made contact with the Maori of New Zealand, he realized that their speciality was not tattooing like the *Te Enata* or making canoes like the Tuamotu. The Maoris were experts at fighting. In a rare episode in the history of European exploration, the indigenous inhabitants of New Zealand won the first skirmish and saw off their European visitors.

Tasman was struck by the forbidding nature of the land when he first viewed the South Island of New Zealand on December 13, 1642. It was dark and rugged, with high mountain ranges that stretched out to the horizon. Rather than possessing welcoming beaches, the steep coast was pounded by great breakers that could reduce the Dutch ships to matchsticks. For four days the Dutch seafarers followed the coast looking for an inlet or bay where they would not be pounded against the shore—a nerve-wracking business for all concerned given the high seas and powerful winds. Finally, they came to a large bay, where they saw smoke rising into the sky.

As Tasman lowered anchor, several canoes set out from the shore. Amid much hollering and blowing of conches and trumpets, the Dutch tried to parley with the island's inhabitants—but to no avail. The Maori, as we now refer to them, were wary and kept their distance. They made no warlike gestures, so the following day Tasman ordered the ships inshore. At the same time, several Maori canoes made their way toward the Europeans, split into two groups, and took station on either side of the flotilla. Suddenly the Maoris whipped out their paddles, rowed like lightning at the boat, and attacked its crew. Three Dutch sailors

BELOW **Abel Tasman found many wondrous locations on his journey through Polynesia and Melanesia, including the Marquess Islands.**

were immediately clubbed to death, one was badly wounded, and the remaining three leaped into the water and swam to safety, covered by gunfire from the Dutch ships.

Soon the water was filled with hostile canoes. Tasman ordered a retreat from what he called Murderers' Bay (now known as Golden Bay) and only just escaped from his pursuers. Tasman stood out to sea. Had the Dutch been able to explore the area in peace he would have realized that the bay lay at the mouth of a large strait that separates the North and South Islands.

Apart from this early failure, Tasman's voyage was spectacularly successful. In 1642 the governor of Dutch Batavia, Anthony van Dieman (1593–1645), decided upon an expedition to search for the "Great South Land" and look for new trading opportunities in the Pacific. He also wanted to find new trade winds that would speed up commerce between Southeast Asia and the Americas. The governor chose Tasman as the leader of two ships, the *Heemskerck* and the *Zeehaen*, and 110 men. The ships were loaded up with many enticing baubles that the Dutch explorers could use to trade for exotic spices and, hopefully, precious metals.

Tasman, ably aided by the noted pilot and surveyor Franchoys Visscher (flourished 1623–45), sailed out of Batavia and headed west to the Indian Ocean. Upon reaching Mauritius, the ships turned south and progressed far into the southern latitudes. Then, with his crew uneasy, the captain decided to turn east and came upon the strong trade winds now known as the "Roaring Forties." These powerful winds propelled the vessels at a fantastic rate back toward the Pacific. Tasman had gone too far to encounter the mainland of Australia, but after many months of sailing, in

November 1642, he came across the tip of a large island below the continent. Tasman first made landfall in the vicinity of what is now known as Macquarie Harbor. This is one of the most forbidding places on Earth, where strong winds whip up from Antarctica and dash freezing water against rocky, hostile shores. During the colonial period, Australia sent the worst criminals to penal settlements in this region to break their spirits and their bodies. Unable to find a place to land, Tasman sent a strong swimmer from the crew to negotiate the waves and claim the new land for Holland.

Continuing up the coast, the two ships were buffeted by strong winds. Only able to take on a small amount of supplies, he picked up the Roaring Forties and proceeded east again. After a week of sailing in the roughest conditions that the crew had ever experienced, they came across New Zealand. Tasman and Franchoys Visscher were elated. So vast did the land seem and so high were the mountains that they were convinced the mission had been accomplished. They named the new land *Staten Landt* in honor of the Dutch Parliament, the States General. The Dutch were convinced it stretched all the way across the Pacific to South America and Cape Horn on the tip of the continent.

Frightened by the hostile Maori (it now appears they were protecting a rich crop), Tasman decided that he had done enough. His exploratory journey had found a fast route to the Pacific and he had discovered the "Great South Land." Turning north for a return journey, the explorers were the first Europeans to come across the Tongan Islands on January 20, 1643. At Tongatapu, in the southermost group of islands in the archipelago, the crew were delighted to find that the Tongans were entirely different from the warlike Maori. For ten days the exhausted Europeans enjoyed the generous hospitality of the locals while they stocked up on fresh fruit, meat, and water. From here the ships sailed on and finally made landfall on the Islands of Fiji. Upon reaching the rough latitude of Batavia, Tasman turned west and headed for home. On the way he discovered much of Melanesia, including New Britain and New Ireland, and also landed on Papua New Guinea.

It had been a remarkable voyage. When he arrived back in Batavia on June 15, 1643, the expedition had circumnavigated Australia in less than ten months, discovered new lands and the Roaring Forties. Despite this, Tasman was disappointed: No new rich markets had been revealed and no new resources found to be plundered. Nevertheless, history was kind to this intrepid explorer, and van Diemen's land was renamed Tasmania in his honor.

BELOW **Tasman's carpenter had to swim through choppy surf before he could place a flag and claim Van Diemen's land for the Dutch. It was later named Tasmania.**

Extinction Events

On both sides of the Pacific, the arrival of humans brought about a cataclysm of extinctions. Large animals known as "megafauna" were particularly vulnerable. In Australia, marsupial megafauna such as diprotodons, giant kangaroos, wombats, and even a huge relative of the Komodo dragon (*Megalania Prisca*) disappeared soon after the arrival of humans.

Similar patterns emerged in the Pacific islands. Nowhere were the extinctions as dramatic when the Maori landed on the islands of Aotearoa (New Zealand). They destroyed an entire array of the large flightless birds known as the moa. There were nine subspecies on the islands when humans landed on their shores in 1200 CE and by 1400 CE they were all extinct except for a remnant population that struggled on for another fifty years in some regions, protected by inhospitable mountainous terrain. Even the largest Moa, which was 10ft tall and weighed 550lb, could not survive the human invasion. It is estimated that 1,500 Polynesian settlers were responsible. DNA evidence indicates that before humans arrived the birds had a diverse genetic gene pool, indicating a healthy and robust population.

Clovis point spearheads

Another unfortunate casualty resulting from these extinctions was Haast's eagle. This was one of the largest raptors to have existed and it was the top carnivore in New Zealand. Maori legends tell of a giant eagle that would descend out of the sky and snap the neck of its victims. The weight of the bird was 33lb and if it was descending at 50mph, it would have the same deadly impact as a large chunk of concrete dropped from an eight-story building.

Seeing that the eagle's main prey was a bipedal bird it may have transferred its attentions to a bipedal human after they arrived—making it necessary for the Maori to hunt them down.

Moa

Jacob Roggeveen

The Mystery of Easter Island

Easter Island was not discovered by Europeans by accident. In 1721 the Dutch explorer Jacob Roggeveen (1659–1729) rounded Cape Horn on the tip of South America and headed into the South Pacific in search of an island known as Davis's Land. An English buccaneer of that name had caught a distant glimpse of the island decades before and Roggeveen wanted to claim it. The Dutchman was unusual in the annals of exploration—he was a trained lawyer, and this was his first expedition, which he was carrying out while he was in his sixties.

It was an ambitious task. Easter Island is one of the most isolated islands in the world and is surrounded by millions of square miles of empty ocean, with its nearest neighbors at least 1,000 miles away. This isolation determined the fate of the inhabitants of Rapa Nui, as they called their homeland.

Finally, after traversing 1,700 miles of empty sea, the Dutchman saw the island looming on the horizon, on Easter Sunday, 1722. He named it *Paasch-Eyland* ("Easter Island.") What he found was entirely unique. Steep cliff-like shores were surmounted by massive heavy-browed statues. Godlike in size, the *moai* stared out to sea. Ranging from 14ft to 70ft high and weighing on average 14 tons, the massive artifacts spoke of a powerful civilization capable of stupendous engineering works.

But here was the mystery that confounded the Dutchman and many subsequent explorers. The island had few navigable beaches and there was no reef to provide an abundance of food. The indigenous inhabitants wore clothes made out of flattened bark and dirt, while what appeared to be jewelry made out of silver was in fact made out of a native parsnip! They grew crops such as sweet potato, taro, and bananas—but there were no trees whatsoever. Large beasts of burden were nonexistent and Roggeveen wondered how the massive stone figures could have been moved to their locations and raised to the vertical. The inhabitants demonstrated no knowledge of the origins or purpose of the *moai*.

Recent research has allowed us to piece together a likely history of this island and explain the stoic structures. The inhabitants of Rapa Nui speak a language similar to that of the Tahitians; the theory is that they made their way from this area to colonize the easternmost point of Polynesia. Soil cores dated to 1200 CE that contain ash give a possible date of arrival for the new inhabitants and point to an early slash-and-burn culture. Also contained in the ancient soil samples are pollens and charcoals from at least twenty-two tree species including a

BELOW **This 1822 print demonstrates that the inhabitants of Easter Island practiced the art of tattooing in common with other Polynesian cultures. Banana leaves are used as decoration.**

relative of the Chilean Wine Palm that can grow as high as 65ft. Other species would have produced abundant crops of fruit and slow-growing hardwoods.

No doubt the first inhabitants used these materials to help them carve out the stone effigies from the volcanic tuff and transport them to their locations. But then environmental catastrophe struck. The project must have exhausted the peoples and their resources. About nine hundred *moai* have been found. Approximately 300 were erected at their current location while the remainder lie abandoned en route to an unknown destination. What caused this collapse? It may have been an overuse of the once-pristine forest until its resources were depleted. Another factor could have been rodents introduced along with the settlers. Feral rats lacking predators may have feasted on the fruits and nuts of the slow-growing trees, a combination of factors that all but destroyed the environment.

Lacking wood to make canoes and separated by thousands of miles of open seas, the inhabitants of Rapa Nui were consigned to an isolated life existing on meager resources. Easter Island lacks natural springs and is subject to frequent droughts. There is evidence that there have been several population crashes. In many caves scattered along the coast are human remains, remains of people that were butchered for their meat. Unable to procure sufficient supplies and beginning to suffer from scurvy, the Dutch soon left the inhabitants of Rapa Nui to their splendid isolation and sailed off to Java.

The Real Robinson Crusoe

Daniel Defoe's book *Robinson Crusoe* (published 1719) is considered to be one of the first novels in English literature. The inspiration for this fascinating tale, which at the time sparked much public interest in the exploration of the Pacific islands, was Scottish sailor Alexander Selkirk (1676–1721). Fearing that the privateer he was aboard, *Cinque Ports*, was going to sink, Selkirk had himself put ashore on a remote island off the coast of Peru named Más a Tierra. (Today it has a different name: In 1966 it was renamed Robinson Crusoe Island.) He was marooned ashore with his sea chest, a bible, a cooking pot, some rum, a musket, and a day's worth of cheese and jam. This was a meager ration indeed—as Selkirk was isolated on his island for four years.

Fortunately for the castaway, the island had been populated with goats by previous European visitors who had also planted an array of vegetables. They had also introduced cats and rats: When the former infested his hut, Selkirk domesticated some of the feral felines by offering them goat meat. Selkirk dressed himself in goat skins and shot the occasional seal for extra food. When he was finally rescued in 1709 by a passing English ship, *The Duke*, he had all but lost the power of speech. And Man Friday, a human helper discovered by the fictional Crusoe on his island? A figment of Defoe's imagination.

LEFT *Robinson Crusoe* was the original bestseller. Based on true events, Daniel Defoe sparked great interest in the Pacific when he published it in 1719.

THE ENGLISH—AND FRENCH— DISCOVER TAHITI

The shores of Tahiti posed a unique danger to seafarers in the eighteenth century. Masters and carpenters had to be on the lookout for pilfering that threatened the very survival of their vessels. Nails that were used to hold together a ship's timbers became a valuable currency.

The discovery of Tahiti on June 19, 1767, by Captain Samuel Wallis (1728–95) of the HMS *Dolphin* was surely one of the most dramatic episodes in the history of exploration. The crew of the HMS *Dolphin* first saw a great cloud-covered mountain rising more than 7,000ft high out of the Pacific Ocean. The steep slopes were covered with verdant jungle fauna, with many streams making their foaming way down perfect tropical beaches to the sea. But as the *Dolphin* steered for the island, it was suddenly engulfed by fog, which cut visibility to almost zero but seemed to amplify the sound of waves breaking on dangerous rocks and reefs. When the fog lifted, the British were confounded to see hundreds of canoes packed with hundreds of warriors between them and the shore.

That the *Dolphin* was the first European vessel to discover Tahiti and the subsequently named Society Islands was something of a miracle. Composed of high islands, features created by volcanic activity, they were the largest landform in the heart of Polynesia. Many explorers such as Magellan and Mendaña had sailed right

BELOW **Queen Oberea of Tahiti decided to form an alliance with the British and ensured that her people respected Captain Wallis and his crewmen.**

ABOVE **In the foreground of this image, a chieftain on a double-hulled canoe urges his tribe to attack the interlopers. They were soon chased off with accurate cannon fire.**

past them, sometimes at less than 100 miles distance. These were no mean coral atolls: It is estimated that 70,000 individuals lived in the two island clusters at the time of European discovery. The mountains, fertile coastline, gentle beaches, reefs, and lagoons provided abundant and rich resources. The weather was comparatively mild, with ocean breezes relieving the heat of the midday sun even though the climate rarely reached the stifling heat of other Polynesian locations. Hurricanes and typhoons were rare visitors to the islands and their bays, making them a perfect stopover for tired mariners.

At first, the indigenous peoples were not entirely sure what to make of the visitors from a distant shore. All Polynesian peoples had similar creation myths: Perhaps they thought that the visitors came from the mythical homeland of *Hawaiki.* Maybe they were an incarnation of the war god Oro? The red coats, flags, and pennants of the British alluded to this god's powers, as did the crashing thunder produced by their powder weapons. Or possibly, and most likely in many islanders' eyes, the British were just humans who possessed a bigger boat than was usual.

For several days, as Wallis sailed around the forty-mile-long island, the indigenous peoples kept track of his movements. Mildly hostile at times and eager to trade fresh food at others, the Tahitians were obviously not sure how to place the English in their frame of reference. When the ships put into Matavai Bay, things came to a head. Hundreds of canoes filled the bay, while a crowd of thousands filled the nearby beaches. Things seemed quite cheerful, and each canoe had a young woman at its prow. The Tahitian maidens often exposed their genitals to the sailors: While the sailors thought this a sexual invitation, it was in fact a part of a ritual by which the women could summon supernatural powers to keep hostile forces at bay. Keen-eyed sailors noticed that the canoes were filled with large and small rocks, and efforts were made to keep them at a distance.

With good reason. A large, double-hulled canoe pulled into the bay. A dignitary clad in flowing red robes thrust a staff into the air. In an immediate response to this signal, hundreds and thousands of rocks were hurled at the British in such numbers that they landed like hail upon the decks. After the initial volley more canoes moved into range before Wallis took decisive action. Cannon, swivel guns, and muskets all crashed out their thunderous response—splitting several canoes in two. The Tahitians tried to move out of killing distance, but, with a range of many hundreds of yards, the heavy shipboard guns could pick off any retreating canoes with impunity. Screaming that the gods had come and were pouring fire and thunder at them, the Tahitians broke up and within thirty minutes the British were in sole occupation of Matavai Bay.

In the face of this demonstration, the Tahitians knew where they stood. Amicable relations were established and powerful Tahitian chiefesses and chiefs made an accommodation with Wallis so that supplies could be obtained for an agreed value. The relations became too amicable. While one or two nails could purchase quite a large amount of food, trading for sexual favors was struck by an inflationary spiral. Sailors were reduced to sleeping on the ship decks as they had pulled out the nails used to suspend their hammocks, and the ship's carpenter reported to the captain that he feared the ship would break up since so many nails had been removed from the hull.

Wallis claimed the island for the crown and named it King George's Island. Not before time. In a remarkable turn of events another European expedition turned up on the island chain that had remained undiscovered for hundreds of years. A French party led by Louis Bougainville (1729–1811) hove into sight of the archipelago on March 22, 1768.

Bougainville was the first French explorer to circumnavigate the Earth. His ground-breaking expedition (1766–69) was the first to carry professional scientists and its aim was to study the biota of the Pacific islands. Naturalists, astronomers, and cartographers made a valuable contribution on the voyage. Unaware that the British had recently claimed the islands, Bougainville named them New Cythera after the location at which the goddess Aphrodite had risen from the sea in ancient Greek mythology. He, too, was struck by the beauty of the women and the carefree lifestyle of the people of Tahiti. Bougainville carried back to France glowing tales of the Tahitian wonderland declaring that the inhabitants were the happiest people on Earth.

On their return journey to France, the expedition came upon the east coast of Australia. Fierce breakers and dangerous reefs forced them to turn aside, costing the French the chance to claim Australia. That honor would fall to the last great explorer of the Pacific—Captain James Cook.

Louis Bougainville

JAMES COOK'S THREE VOYAGES

Captain James Cook

Several hundred years of uncoordinated exploration of the Pacific ensured that European knowledge of the ocean was patchy at best. The three expeditions of Englishman James Cook changed all that. Born in Yorkshire in 1728, he was a superior navigator, a brilliant cartographer, and an experienced seaman. Cook revolutionized the understanding of the Pacific.

His first voyage was perhaps the greatest. Setting out in the converted collier HMS *Endeavour* on August 5, 1768, this expedition was commissioned to observe the transit of Venus from Tahiti and collect biological specimens under the aegis of Sir Joseph Banks. The readings of Venus were made on Tahiti in June 1769.

Cook then made his way to New Zealand. Fortunately, he took a translator named Tupaia from Tahiti and, able to communicate with the Maoris, ensured that he was welcomed by the fierce tribesmen. Cook's remarkable charts of the New Zealand coast still exist: He was able to prove that New Zealand was an archipelago, not part of the "Great South Land" and that the Cook Strait separated the two main islands.

Cook's achievements continued to mount. Following old charts from Abel Tasman, Cook was the first European to reach Australia's fertile east coast. Here he proved the existence of Bass Strait separating the mainland of Australia from Tasmania, before discovering Botany Bay and claiming the entire east coast for the British Crown—and naming it New South Wales. Joseph Banks collected thousands of specimens in this part of the journey and was the first to declare that the bay would make an ideal place for a colony. The unique Australian plant the Banksia is named after this remarkable figure. Sailing northward, HMS *Endeavour* was the first ship to navigate the Great Barrier Reef.

Rounding the northernmost tip of Australia, which he named Cape York, Cook passed through the Torres Strait—proving that Papua New Guinea and Australia were separate. After sailing through the Dutch East Indies, around the Cape of Good Hope, and home, the first expedition ended in July 1771.

Rations under Cook's watch were plentiful. Each sailor could expect in his daily ration of around 1lb of biscuit, a share of alcohol made up of beer, wine, or grog, and 1lb of salted pork or beef. Part of the weekly ration was 2 pints of dried peas, a bag of oatmeal, and 1lb of dairy—cheese or butter. Although vitamins had not yet been discovered, experienced captains such as Cook laid in as much fresh fruit and vegetables as possible, such as citrus fruits and cabbages as a remedy for scurvy. When Cook put into Madeira each man of the HMS *Endeavour* was issued with 20lb of raw onions!

Ship's rations

By the latter half of the eighteenth century, deaths from scurvy were much rarer. When Commodore Arthur Phillip (1738–1814) led the First Fleet from Portsmouth to Botany Bay over an eleven-month period in 1787–88, only forty-two individuals died out of almost 1,500 hundred passengers and crew. None died of scurvy; they succumbed to other injuries or illnesses.

Over the next two voyages (1772–75 and 1776–80) Cook's achievements were remarkable. He searched for the Northwest Passage and penetrated further north than any previous explorer below the Arctic Circle. Several new lands were discovered, including the Pitcairn Islands and New Caledonia. He visited most islands of the Pacific, including Tahiti, Tonga, the Marquesas, Easter Island, New Georgia, the South Sandwich Islands, and Hawaii. It was here that the great explorer met his fate.

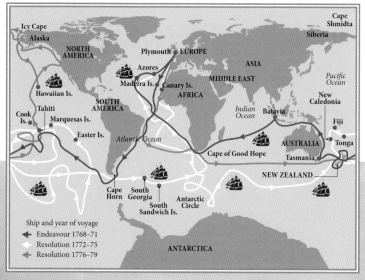

LEFT AND BELOW Captain Cook's voyages created a remarkable record of exploration throughout the Pacific. Increasingly irascible, during his third voyage, Cook made a fatal error.

Cook and the Cannibals

Through his journeys mapping and exploring the New Zealand islands, Captain Cook was able to prove beyond doubt that the Maori were engaged in cannibal practices. At Ship Cove, a Lieutenant Clarke took the head of a young Maori killed while engaged in a tribal skirmish to the HMS *Endeavour*. In the interests of science, the lieutenant cut a couple of slices from the face and grilled it on the galley fire before offering the choice morsels to a couple of Maori—who devoured the meat with obvious relish. They repeated the experiment when Cook and two scientists were there to witness it and several of the crew members vomited in revulsion.

Cook's journal describes how as they explored the islands more signs of cannibalism began to emerge. Two young men from one tribe joined the expedition, but when Cook tried to put them ashore, they remonstrated with him saying they would surely be cooked and eaten, as the tribe inhabiting that part of the coast were considered their enemies. They also came upon some native ovens filled with human remains.

The explorers also came upon some Maori engaged in a feast. The clan was engaged with picking the half-cooked flesh from human bones with their

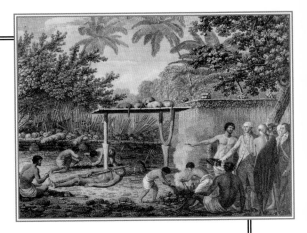

ABOVE **Cook and his party observe Tahitians prepare a man and several pigs for sacrifice in one of the sacred enclosures common throughout Polynesia.**

sharp teeth that had been filed into points. Baskets were around the campsite filled with bones showing bits of gristle still attached but with clear bite marks. Cook's interpreters were able to shed light on where the grisly feast had been obtained. A canoe with seven members of an opposing tribe had been swept into the inlet, where the twelve Maori present at the feast had clubbed and killed them. This had happened five days before Cook's visit, so the small clan of twelve people had eaten seven people in that short time. The heads had been removed from the bodies and all displayed large holes through which the brains had been extracted. Joseph Banks, the expedition's botanist, was able to purchase one of the heads but the clan refused to sell any others.

Captain Cook's Death

On February 4, after around a month on Hawaii, Cook felt that his small fleet had enough provisions for the rest of the trip. He bid the Hawaiians farewell. They had been treated well. It was, after all, the Hawaiian season of *Makahiki*. During this time peace reigned throughout the islands and it was forbidden to make war upon your neighbors.

Unfortunately, gale force winds forced the expedition to return to Kealakekua Bay. The crew immediately noticed that the mood of the indigenous people had shifted. *Makahiki* was over. While not overtly hostile, the locals began pilfering stores. Metal was the most prized booty, and when a Hawaiian took off with a blacksmith's tongs three sailors followed in pursuit. They were forced back by a mass of angry, jeering men hurling stones. Cook ordered his marines to reload their fine shot with musket balls, but the final straw came on February 14. A longboat went missing and Cook was determined to recover it. He led a party of marines and sailors onshore and remonstrated with the local chieftain for its return. The Hawaiians made a move to attack and Cook retaliated by firing his musket, but it was not enough to fend off the furious Hawaiians who soon overwhelmed the landing party.

Cook discharged his musket and then swung it around like a club in a desperate attempt at self-defence. He was struck with a war club on the back of the head before being stabbed. As befitted a great chief, Cook was immediately eviscerated and dismembered. The Hawaiians believed that whoever possessed the remains of such a great chieftain would inherit his bravery. After a standoff that lasted several days, the Hawaiians returned some of the captain's remains. They were placed in a weighted box that was dropped to the bottom of Kealakekua Bay, although some of his arm and leg bones, his jaw, and his scalp remained with the Hawaiians.

Kalani'ōpu'u, the ruling chief of the island of Hawaii

Despite his dreadful end, Cook's achievements were truly remarkable. His scientific voyages, the detail of his cartography, and his description of prevailing winds and tides far outstripped the achievements of his predecessors. Cook's remarkable ethnographic studies of the Pacific people gave Europeans a tremendous understanding of the once mysterious lands of the Pacific Ocean.

RIGHT **Cook had outstayed his welcome by the time Kalani'ōpu'u struck the blow that brought him down. The explorer's body parts were divided among Hawaiian chieftains.**

6

CONQUERING AMERICA AND AUSTRALIA

IN ABOUT 150 CE PTOLEMY OF ALEXANDRIA, a Greek astronomer and cartographer, drew a map of the world. He drew a large imaginary continent below Eurasia, which later came to be called *Terra Australis Incognita*— the unknown south land. Much of the exploration of the Pacific was designed to find this mythical land— the "Great Southern Land" (see Chapter 5).

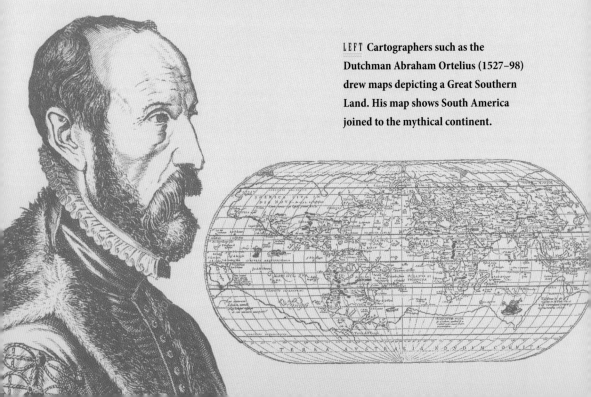

LEFT **Cartographers such as the Dutchman Abraham Ortelius (1527–98) drew maps depicting a Great Southern Land. His map shows South America joined to the mythical continent.**

AUSTRALIA AND THE PACIFIC

The first encounters with Australia were almost accidental. Dutch sailors had two ways of getting to Jakarta across the Indian Ocean. After rounding the Cape of Good Hope, they could proceed north past Madagascar and Ceylon (Sri Lanka) and then southeast to the island of Java. In the early seventeenth century a much faster route became available: After passing the tip of Africa, the mariners proceeded south and caught the "Roaring Forties"—strong and constant winds sweeping along the Fortieth Latitude. After gauging that their longitudinal bearings were in line with Java, the trading vessels would turn north. Gauging latitude by dead reckoning was a tricky business and should the navigators make a mistake, their ships would run straight into Australia.

Dutch sailor Dirk Hartog (1580–1621) was the first European to discover the barren and rugged west coast of Australia. In 1616 his ship the *Eendracht* was blown too far east and came upon some islands near Shark Bay in modern western Australia. A party went ashore to what is now known as Dirk Hartog Island and affixed a pewter plate to a post.

ABOVE Dirk Hartog's pewter plate dated to October 25th, 1616, was recently discovered in Western Australia.

A decade earlier, in 1606, another Dutch navigator, Willem Janszoon (1570–1630), was dispatched from the Dutch East Indies to find New Guinea, a land reputedly filled with gold. He discovered that the tropical coasts of New Guinea and the Gulf of Carpentaria were harsh terrain filled with hostile indigenous warriors. Dutch seafarer and merchant Abel Tasman, in 1644, and in 1688, William Dampier (1651–1715), an English sailor who was the first person to circumnavigate the world three times, charted more of the rugged coastline of north and west Australia. Both found little to recommend the new land—now called Australia by the Dutch—for settlement. It was only when Englishman Captain James Cook explored the fertile east coast of Australia in 1770 that Europeans took an active interest in the new land. Even now, 80 percent of Australians live on the narrow east coast of the island continent.

BELOW Captained by Willem Janszoon, the *Duyfken* was used to explore northern Australia including the Gulf of Carpentaria.

"AUSTRALIA FELIX"

Gregory Blaxland

Australia was settled by Commodore Arthur Phillip on January 26, 1788, when he claimed the southern continent as a British possession. For the next three decades, explorers and settlers colonized the rich farmlands of the Sydney Basin. But the imposing barrier of the Blue Mountains prevented further expansion. Part of the Great Dividing Range that stretches right down the Australian coast, the Blue Mountains—while not very tall—are a maze of steep valleys interspersed with impassable clefts and cliffs or forest-covered peaks. Even today, much of this rugged terrain remains unexplored. As recently as 1994, rock climbers descended into an unexplored valley that had never before seen a human presence. Hidden in the valley's depths was the last stand of the Wollemi Pine—an ancient tree that was only known from the fossil record and first evolved more than 200 million years ago.

By 1810, population pressures and the demand for new farming land meant that the colony had to extend beyond the mountain barriers if it was to survive. Many had tried to cross the barrier by following stream and river valleys but these had always come to a dead end.

Australia's first great land explorers set out to cross the barrier in 1813. English-born pioneer Gregory Blaxland (1778–1853) decided that the best way to cross the mountains was to find a plateau and follow it to the west. With him were William Lawson (1774–1850) and William Wentworth (1790–1872), both considered to be accomplished bushmen. The men took four convicts, four horses, and five dogs to help in their quest. For two weeks they were taxed to their limit while hacking their way through thick bush. Unable to see beyond the dense foliage, the

BELOW **Even though Blaxland's journey of exploration was quite short, it was a momentous event in Australian history.**

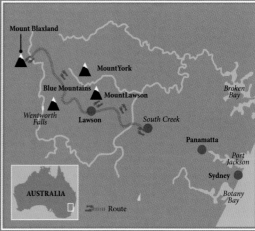

party cut symbols into the trees they passed so that they could retrace their steps when necessary. One dog managed to hunt down a kangaroo, a vital addition to their stocks of salt beef, which were quickly running out. Finally, they reached Mount York and, looking down, saw lush plains and grasslands stretching off into the distance. By cutting hoofmarks for the horses, the exhausted party managed to descend the steep slope of Mount York into a fertile region of streams, rivers, and pasture—enough, in Blaxland's words, to sustain the colony for thirty years.

Convicts were soon set to work building a road across the mountains allowing settlers to sally forth to exploit the new territory. Unhappy with the seizure of their traditional lands, the indigenous Australians were often hostile to future explorers. Scottish-born surveyor and explorer Major Thomas Mitchell (1792–1855) adopted the unfortunate policy of shooting first and asking questions later.

A veteran of the Napoleonic Wars, Mitchell was appointed Surveyor-General of New South Wales in 1828. From 1831 to 1836 he led several expeditions into the New South Wales hinterland and turned south to cross the Murray River, before penetrating into the fertile regions of modern Victoria. Only seeing the indigenous Australians as hostile nomads, Mitchell failed to realize that they had managed the fertile grasslands interspersed with copses of native trees using firestick farming that ensured their favorite prey animal, the kangaroo, was attracted to the rich grazing lands. Mitchell's reports of an *Australia Felix* ("Fortunate Australia") ensured that new settlers were soon flocking to the newly explored lands. The Major Mitchell's cockatoo is named in his honor.

Major Mitchell's cockatoo

BELOW Beyond the Blue Mountains, vast swathes of fertile farmland was opened up to new settlers. Tribes of indigenous Australians were disposed of their ancestral lands.

The Accidental Explorer

Truth is often stranger than fiction. This saying couldn't be more apt than in the case of William Buckley (1780–1856), a British convict who was part of an exploratory expedition and settlement in Port Phillip Bay in southern Australia in 1803. Buckley was hard to miss—more than 6ft tall, he had a shock of bright red hair and pale skin. Despite this, he managed to escape his jailers and flee into the Australian wilderness on foot. He circumnavigated the entire bay and ended up living among the indigenous peoples of the Bellarine Peninsula.

Just before Buckley met the local clan, he found a spear stuck into a warrior's burial mound. The escaped convict thought it might come in handy and pulled it out of the grave. Almost immediately afterward, he came across a war party from the local Wadawurrung tribe. The indigenous peoples of Port Phillip believed that ghosts were pale-skinned, with red hair— when they saw the escaped convict clutching their comrade's spear they presumed it was the dead warrior returned as a ghost. The tribe adopted the tall Englishman and for the next thirty years he lived among the Wadawurrung, exploring all around Port Phillip. When another expedition arrived in Port Phillip in 1835, they were amazed to find a 6ft-tall red-haired indigenous Australian clad in kangaroo skins and wielding a boomerang.

Buckley proved to be an invaluable guide and translator for the new settlers—although it took him several weeks to remember English. His name is now part of the Australian vernacular—"Buckley's chance" refers to something that requires a huge amount of luck to survive.

BELOW **William Buckley caused quite a stir when he was reunited with European settlers after living with the aboriginals for more than thirty years.**

THE RED CENTER

Once the east coast and its immediate hinterland had been explored, several mysteries remained. What lay at the heart of the mighty continent and was there an inland sea fed by rivers pouring off the Great Dividing Range? Charles Sturt (1795–1869) was determined to find the great inland sea of Australia—instead he found drought, starvation, and scurvy.

Born in Bengal, India, Sturt joined the army and saw service in Spain, Canada, and Ireland. When his Thirty-Ninth Regiment of Foot was posted to Australia in 1826, he fell in love with the wild bushland of England's latest colony and in 1828 set out on his first expedition across the Blue Mountains, going on to penetrate hundreds of miles into the interior.

In 1829, Sturt set off again and found the Murrumbidgee River. The party built a 27ft boat and set off downstream until they encountered the largest river in Australia: the Murray, continuing until they reached a large ocean estuary. The expedition then had to sail and row 900 miles up the river system back to Sydney during the year 1830. This expedition made Sturt a hero and opened up the southeast corner of Australia to settlement. Adelaide, the capital of South Australia, would be founded at the mouth of the Murray River.

In 1844, his last expedition sailed up the Darling River before setting off to the northwest, into the heart of Australia. The sixteen-strong party rode into a blistering drought, where temperatures reached 130°F and water holes disappeared. Trapped in an environment as hostile as the Earth's poles, the party had to dig underground shelters to stay cool and there they stewed for six months until rain finally arrived. Sturt and four hardy colleagues then pushed on for another 450 miles until they came to the vast central Simpson Desert. Seeing no sign of an inland sea, the party turned for home—and the scurvy-ridden explorers staggered into Adelaide in January 1846. Almost blind and carried on a stretcher, Sturt was lucky to survive.

ABOVE **While no inland seas were discovered beyond the Great Dividing Range, the vast river system based on the Murray River was found.**

BURKE AND WILLS

Irishman Robert O'Hara Burke (1821–61) and Englishman William John Wills (1834–61) were chosen by the Royal Society of Victoria to lead an expedition to explore the center of Australia and find a route to lay an overland telegraph line connecting the north and south of the continent.

Before the expedition set out, Burke had proved himself an excellent soldier and an efficient policeman. His success at administering some of the gold diggings during the 1850s ensured he had a high profile in the colonial outpost of Victoria. Yet while Burke was an efficient administrator, he was a poor choice as an explorer. His deputy Wills was an experienced surveyor, but like his superior, no bushman.

When Burke set out on August 20th, 1860, he had planned for every possible contingency. The vast cavalcade that traversed the center of Melbourne incorporated twenty-four camels and many horse-drawn wagons carrying around 21 tons of supplies, and was accompanied by geologists, artists, naturalists, botanists, and Afghan camel drivers. It slowly made its way north, and after three long months had only

BELOW Burke and Wills were the first to cross the Australian continent from North to South. Death was their only reward.

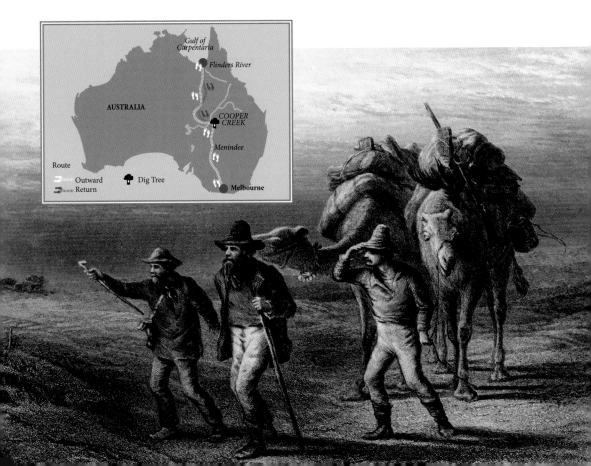

managed to traverse one-quarter of the expected journey when it reached Menindee. Even at this early stage in the journey, Burke was beginning to alienate many of the party with his high-handed and strong-willed manner.

Desperate to speed things up, Burke split up his party and headed off to Cooper Creek in October. The man he appointed to bring up the main supplies was incompetent and did not appear at the planned rendezvous. Burke then made another potentially fatal error. He decided to make a dash for the Gulf of Carpentaria in mid-December—the hottest part of the year. He left a party at Cooper Creek under the command of William Brahe (1835–1912) with orders to wait three months and then set off back to Melbourne if Burke and the others had not returned. With six camels and one horse Burke, Wills, and two other men set off. Wills, shocked at Burke's decision, secretly implored Brahe to wait an additional month. After spending two months traversing some of the most hostile terrain on the planet while sweltering in temperatures of up to 140°F, the party reached the Gulf of Carpentaria. Burke and Wills became the first Europeans to traverse the continent from south to north.

Burke would not be able to enjoy the renown of his accomplishment. The members of the party turned and retraced their steps, but by this time were in a dreadful state. Supplies were exhausted, their camels were dead, and—worst of all—Burke saw indigenous people as a hostile presence and did not learn how to obtain bush tucker. Weather conditions had shifted dramatically and the group had to contend with flash floods and savage electrical storms. They abandoned all but their most precious kit. When the poor diet took its toll and one of the explorers, Scottish-born former sailor named Charlie Gray, died from dysentery, Burke made a fateful decision. They would rest for a day and give their comrade a decent Christian burial. On April 21, 1861, the three survivors returned to Cooper Creek—eight hours after Brahe and the other members had left carrying off most of the remaining supplies.

Isabella Bird

Australia's inhospitable landscape was not just for male travelers. Isabella Bird (1831–1904) was a remarkable explorer who spent her life indulging her love of exploration. In 1872, she left Scotland for Australia in the hope that the dry heat would help with her health issues. However, she found the climate did not suit her, and so moved on to Hawaii before heading on a trip through the Pacific which ended up in the American Rockies. Here she traversed 800 miles of barely explored wilderness in 1873, before going on to visit India and the Far East.

ABOVE **Isabella Bird Bishop wrote tremendously successful travelogues, the most popular of which was one based on her time in Hawaii.**

An Enduring Mystery—The Fate of Ludwig Leichhardt

Ludwig
Leichhardt

Prussian naturalist Ludwig Leichhardt (1813–c. 48) was an unusual explorer. Leichhardt studied medicine in Berlin and London before emigrating to Australia in 1841. Something of a prickly fellow, he found comfort in the solitude of Australia and explored the east coast. In 1844–45 he traveled from Brisbane to the Gulf of Carpentaria in far-off Arnhem Land. The plucky German was awarded a gold medal from the London and Paris geographical societies in 1847 for his acute observation of the indigenous peoples, along with the land and the flora among which they thrived.

Two years later, he set off on another journey: To cross the entire desert continent from east to west. Even today this is a hazardous undertaking. When the explorer set out on a 2,800-mile journey through the heart of the unknown land, many thought he might not return.

Even though the expedition took seven men, twenty mules, fifty bullocks, and huge amounts of supplies, it vanished without trace— leading to one of the greatest mysteries of the history of exploration.

The expedition set out in March 1848 from the Condamine River and was last seen on the Darling Downs in central New South Wales in April that year, then vanished. Search parties funded by governments and wealthy individuals were dispatched in the 1850s, but not a shoe, not a pot, not even a bone from the expedition was found. One rumor got back to the east coast telling of a very old white man with a long yellow beard living with the outback tribe and some romantic souls thought this might be the missing Prussian.

Only one possible relic has been found. In 1900 an indigenous Australian stockman found a rough brass plate inscribed with the explorer's name, dated 1848. It had been attached to Leichhardt's gun when he had set off and despite being fire-damaged was still adhering to part of the weapon. It was jammed into a Boab tree and a large "L" was inscribed in the tree's trunk, a common practice among Australian explorers.

Found in Sturt Creek on the northern fringe of West Australia's Great Sandy Desert, it suggests that the explorers covered at least two-thirds of their planned journey. Beyond that, nothing is known of the Prussian's fate.

North America

North America is a huge continent. It covers almost 10 million square miles and different climate zones stretch from the frozen Artic near the North Pole to the sweltering desert climes of Arizona and the tropical humidity of Mexico. With such vast spaces to be covered, it is no wonder that European exploration lasted for hundreds of years. During the sixteenth and seventeenth centuries, many explorers penetrated into the continent from the Spanish-held territories to the south or through the wild lands of the Canadian mountains. In the eighteenth and nineteenth centuries, the main impetus for exploration came from the increasingly densely populated eastern seaboard, as settlers and governments sought to expand westward into the lands held by a plethora of indigenous peoples. These later explorers paved the way for the great westward treks that saw the final states added to the American nation.

The French Lend a Hand

In the mid-1600s, French explorers had traversed many parts of North America, continuing the work of men such as Spanish conquistador Hernando de Soto a hundred years earlier.

Notable among these were Louis Jolliet (c. 1645–1700) and Jacques Marquette (1637–75). Hearing tales of the mighty Mississippi River and hoping that it would provide a quick route to China, the two Frenchmen led an expedition with five others southward from St. Ignace on the north bank of Lake Michigan. Warned by indigenous tribes that the inhabitants of the Mississippi region were violent, the small expedition nevertheless set off in canoes and by June 1673, had reached the waters of the vast river. For 1,000 miles the explorers traveled downriver, finding little threat from the local tribes. Then, after establishing that the river emptied into the Gulf of Mexico, the party turned back.

René-Robert Cavelier (1643–87) explored and claimed for the French crown much of the Mississippi, Illinois, and Ohio river basins. Cavelier named this huge territory Louisiana after French king Louis XIV (reigned 1643–1715) in 1682. With these lands the French had an important stake in North America.

BELOW Father Jacques Marquette waves a peace pipe to assure the indigenous inhabitants of the Mississippi that he came with good intentions.

Conquest of the West: Across the Appalachians— Daniel Boone

Today travelers driving from North Carolina through to Kentucky or West Virginia may have to slow down on the occasional tight turn, but they can usually traverse the Appalachian Mountains within a matter of hours without having to leave the climate-controlled comfort of their vehicle. But for the early settlers on the eastern coast of North America the Appalachians were a formidable barrier that prevented expansion into the rich farmland beyond, the bluegrass region of central Kentucky, and on to the vast plains westward. But just as enterprising explorers crossed the Blue Mountains in Australia, so adventurous travelers eventually made light of the Appalachians too.

Daniel Boone (1734–1820) was born to an English Quaker family in Pennsylvania. In the forested lands surrounding the family home, the young Boone developed good hunting skills. The family moved to the Yadkin River settlement nestled in the foothills of the Appalachians in the state of North Carolina. In 1755, Boone served with the British in the French and Indian War, honing his skills as a frontiersman and fighter. After the war, Boone returned home and seemed to settle down to connubial bliss with his wife Rebecca Bryan.

After a few failed solo expeditions into the Appalachians, in 1769 a comrade from the wars, John Findley, asked Boone to escort him across the mountains. Boone jumped at the chance. Setting out with four other men, the pair found what is now known as the Cumberland Gap. This took them into a fertile paradise filled with animals such as buffalo and turkeys plus a vast acreage of potential farmland drained by the Kentucky and Ohio rivers. They traced these rivers as far as modern Louisville and accumulated a hoard of valuable pelts. Unfortunately, the party was then robbed by a gang of Cherokee. Thanks to his experience in the Indian wars, Boone was able to communicate with the locals and escape with his life.

In 1775, Boone was placed in charge of a surveying party and was able to map out the Wilderness Road across the Appalachians, down to what is now the state of Kentucky. The first European settlement was named Boonesboro after the indefatigable explorer—a rough collection of wooden huts surrounded by a primitive but effective stockade. The settlers fought off several attacks from the indigenous Shawnee tribes, and Boone's status as a hunter and frontiersman reached almost mythical proportions among the settlers and the indigenous tribes. Even as late as 1799 Boone maintained his wanderlust and led a party of settlers into the wilds of Missouri in a search for new lands.

Daniel Boone

Meriwether Lewis and William Clark

On November 2, 1804, American explorers Meriwether Lewis (1774–1809) and William Clark (1770–1838) noticed that the Columbia River, which they were following through the Cascade Mountains, was ebbing and flowing with the tides of the Pacific Ocean. The pair knew that their journey across the North American continent would soon be over. One of the greatest land grabs in history could proceed.

ABOVE Lewis and Clark take a break while traversing the Columbia River.

A year before, President Thomas Jefferson (1743–1826) had purchased 828,000 square miles of American land known as the Louisiana Territory from French First Consul (later emperor) Napoleon Bonaparte. For the measly sum of $15 million, the United States had more than doubled in size.

But Jefferson then had to prove that Americans could explore and possess the new lands and unite the entire continent southward of the British lands of Canada. This was how Lewis and Clark found themselves on the Columbia River. The president commanded his personal secretary, Meriwether Lewis, to lead a team of explorers from American territory to the Pacific Ocean. Clark was chosen as the co-leader.

Jefferson created the "Corps of Discovery" and had Lewis undergo significant training to prepare him for the role of its leader. He was sent to Philadelphia to learn geology, geography, cartography, and even zoology.

Lewis was instructed to make accurate maps of the regions the explorers would traverse and take particular note of significant landmarks, soil types, and the tribes they encountered. Thirty-six experienced soldiers and frontiersmen were recruited to aid the expedition and no expense was spared procuring gifts for the indigenous

Prairie dog

peoples they would meet; they carried the latest scientific instruments including compasses, a chronometer, sextants, thermometers, and other surveying equipment.

In 1803, the expedition set out from Washington, D.C., and by May 1804 was traveling up the Missouri having just left St. Louis. By September they had reached what is now known as South Dakota, and the leaders recorded with amazement the huge herds of buffalo, deer, and antelope that roamed the rich prairie lands. They were particularly impressed with the vast buffalo herds that could be 50 miles long and 25 miles wide.

In November 1804, the party wintered in what is now North Dakota. Crucial to Lewis and Clark's success was their peaceful interactions with the indigenous tribes whose territory they passed through. This success was largely due to Sacagawea, a young woman who joined the expedition in 1804. The Shoshone woman was both a guide and a translator who helped the expedition navigate several tricky situations. Finally, on August 12, 1805, they reached the Lemhi Pass through the Rocky Mountains. Here they recognized that the party had crossed the Continental divide, the line where some rivers headed east toward the plains while others drained into the Pacific. Months trekking through the wilderness followed, and with the assistance of the Sacagawea, the party caught sight of what they thought was the Pacific Ocean (but was actually just an estury) on November 7, 1805.

The group retraced their steps east, arriving back in St. Louis on September 23, 1806. They had made a remarkable journey, although it seemed not to have brought much, if any, satisfaction to Lewis. He either died by suicide or was murdered on October 11, 1809, while traveling to Washington, D. C. in order to try to recoup expenses from the expedition.

The discovery of gold in California in the 1840s and in Indian territories in the 1870s effectively opened up the last of the North American continent to exploration and settlement by Europeans.

LEFT **John Charles Fremont (1813–90) was another great American explorer. Many modern American states were explored by him. Here he lays claim to the Rocky Mountains.**

The Last Undiscovered Lands

Despite the fact that explorers crisscrossed the deserts of Australia, the vast wildernesses there ensured that some indigenous Australian tribes knew next to nothing of the new culture that had colonized most of their continent. The Martu tribe, after being horribly maltreated when the Canning Stock Route was established in 1906, continued to keep their distance from European settlers. Until this modern intervention, they had lived in the Great Sandy Desert, practicing their hunter-gathering ways for thousands of years, using well-worn tracks etched by hundreds of generations of their forefathers.

One fierce tribe has resisted proper contact with modern civilization: Any explorers who reach their lands are quickly speared to death or shot by arrows! Around 750 miles from the Indian mainland is a tiny landmass of just 23 square miles known as North Sentinel Island. Between fifty and 150 people make up the Sentinelese population and they speak their own language, which is thousands of years old. They pursue a hunter-gatherer lifestyle and have no contact with the outside world. Although theoretically a part of the Indian state, the tribe is entirely autonomous and the government does not visit the island

ABOVE Isolated tribes of the Amazon River basin are still prepared to defend their ancient way of life from encroaching development.

for fear of infecting the inhabitants with modern diseases. It is illegal to come within 3 nautical miles of the island, and even taking photos of these mysterious people is now forbidden. In late 2018 an American missionary who tried to make contact was killed by the Sentinelese firing arrows.

In the Amazon rainforest of Brazil, residing in the western states of Mato Grosso and Rondonia, there are between eighty and 100 tribes. The Brazilian government used to try to contact these isolated communities, but now just do flyovers so as not to impact the tribes' health. Any helicopters going down to take a closer look are usually met by a barrage of arrows shot out of the forest.

7 UNLOCKING AFRICA

BY THE END OF THE EIGHTEENTH CENTURY, most of the inhabited regions of the world had been mapped by Europeans. Only Africa remained a true mystery. But this would not last for long.

The imperial powers cast covetous eyes over the continent's potentially rich territories, while Christian missionaries saw a vast and fertile field for conversions. And by the early nineteenth century a new motivation emerged: Africa was the source of most of the world's slaves; some Europeans, and in particular the English, saw it as their moral duty to stamp out this pernicious and evil trade.

LEFT **David Livingstone fought illness, wild animals, and personal tragedy in his travels across Africa. He never lost his humanity and respect for the locals.**

THE BEGINNING OF EUROPEAN EXPLORATION OF AFRICA

In June 1788, a group of English dignitaries, including the respected botanist Joseph Banks (1743–1820), sat down to supper at St. Alban's Tavern in London. Many were influential members of the Royal Geographical Society. The members of this powerful group had one thing on their minds: the interior of the vast African continent.

A small glimmer of light was shone on this vast interior when James Bruce (1730–94) set out to find the source of the Nile. The pugnacious, flame-haired Scot penetrated deep into the mysterious lands of Egypt and the Sudan and proceeded into Ethiopia, where the rulers of the Abyssinian empire held court. One custom that Bruce described in his memoirs was particularly brutal: Warriors returning from a victorious battle would shower the emperor with testicles taken from the defeated enemies.

Determined to capitalize on the newfound interest in the continent, Banks and his cronies established the African Association, a body devoted to the study of Africa. The Confederation of Germany (it did not become a nation until 1871) was "the new kid on the block" as far as empire building was concerned, but the increasingly industrialized and powerful proto-nation also took a hand in African exploration. The country's Geographical Society sent out hundreds of German explorers. Heinrich Barth (1821–65), Erwin von Bary (1846–77), Adolf Bastian (1826–1905), the Swiss Johann Ludwig Burckhardt (1784–1817), Baron Karl Klaus von der Decken (1833–65), and Alexander Freiherr von Humboldt (1769–1859) were just some of the exploratory luminaries to set out across the mysterious continent.

BELOW Joseph Banks was not content with the achievements he made when accompanying Captain Cook. He was determined to open up Africa to English exploration.

Barth was a tremendously important explorer who carried his academic brilliance in history, geography, archeology, and linguistics into the field. Joining a British expedition in 1850, Barth was the first to observe the intricate rock paintings in the Hoggar mountains right in the middle of the Sahara Desert. These paintings, which showed animals usually seen in African wetlands such as crocodiles and hippopotami, suggested to the fascinated explorers that the Sahara was once covered in lush, almost tropical vegetation. Barth's detailed notes on the civilizations and terrain that he encountered did much to shed light on this mysterious region.

THE SAHARA AND GORDON LAING

Alexander Gordon Laing

For hundreds of years, Arab and Tuareg trading caravans had crisscrossed the immense inhospitable sands of the Sahara. By the time Europeans turned their eyes to this desert that covers 3.6 million square miles, these fierce warriors were another danger that had to be faced.

Alexander Gordon Laing (1793–1826) was one of the first Europeans to face their fury. Timbuktu was once a trading center controlling the immense wealth that flowed from sub-Saharan Africa to the Mediterranean and the Middle East. While the importance of this city had faded somewhat, Europeans still considered it to be the African equivalent of El Dorado, the fabled South American city of gold (see Chapter 3). Laing was chosen by the British government to cross the Sahara and find the legendary city.

On July 16, 1825, Laing set off on his remarkable journey. Things seemed to be going well until they were set upon by fierce Tuareg warriors. Only Laing survived, although his wounds were quite horrific: He had five saber cuts on the crown of his head, three on the left temple, five slashes to his right arm and hand, three to his left, a fractured jaw, an ear hanging by a thread of flesh, and a "dreadful gash" on the back of his neck from a blow that had almost nicked his windpipe!

Despite this, he struggled on and entered Timbuktu on August 18, 1826. Here the inhabitants treated the white man with respect. It was respect mingled with fear. The fear of armed Christians imposing their will on new territories and British attempts to curtail the lucrative slave trade meant that Europeans were less than welcome. Rumors circulated that Laing was a Christian spy. A friendly sheikh warned Laing of a plot to take his life and in September 1826 the Englishman made to leave. Too late. On the outskirts of Timbuktu Laing was beaten to death by his guide.

RIGHT Convinced that Laing was a spy determined to interfere with the slave trade, his guide was ordered to assassinate his employer.

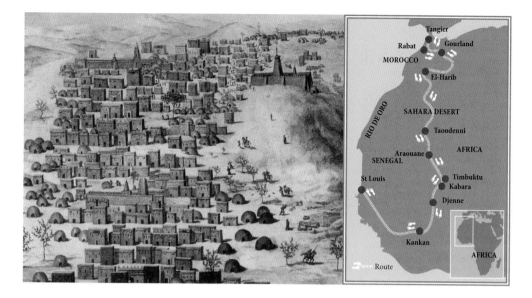

Map labels: Tangier, Rabat, Gourland, MOROCCO, El-Harib, RIO DE ORO, SAHARA DESERT, Taoudenni, AFRICA, Araouane, SENEGAL, St Louis, Timbuktu, Kabara, Djenne, Kankan, AFRICA, Route

René Caillié

Two years later French explorer Auguste René Caillié (1799–1838) entered Timbuktu but lived to tell the tale. He ensured that he was disguised as an Arab. The Geographical Society of Paris was enamored of the idea of finding Timbuktu and put up a 10,000-franc prize for the first European to enter the city. Caillié had been brought up on tales of adventure: His favorite read was Daniel Defoe's 1719 novel *Robinson Crusoe*. At the age of sixteen, the young Frenchman left home and joined an expedition to Senegal. For the next decade he lived in Africa, learning local languages and customs. In 1827, Caillié accepted the challenge to find Timbuktu and he set off from the Dakar region of the west coast of Africa. Passing though modern Guinea, the Frenchman navigated the Niger River until he came upon Timbuktu in what we now call Mali.

ABOVE Like many Europeans Caillie was disappointed when he reached Timbuktu. He barely survived the journey home across the Sahara.

Caillié's entry went unnoticed by the locals. Dressed as an Arab with headgear that shaded his pale face, the cunning Frenchman used a hollowed-out copy of the *Koran* to hide his expedition notes. In April 1828, he entered the city but found it to be a tremendous disappointment. Mud huts dotted over a sandy plane with a few tatty mosques: No El Dorado. After two weeks he begged his way onto an Arab caravan and crossed the Sahara, traveling almost due north to Tangier on the Mediterranean coast. Although he was not the first European to enter Timbuktu, Caillié was awarded the 10,000-franc prize and wrote a best-seller telling of his adventures.

Despite their varied fates, both explorers had demonstrated that the Sahara could be crossed and recorded many of the most important features of the vast desert.

DEADLY DISEASES

Mosquito: yellow fever

EUROPEAN EXPLORERS had to contend with many deadly diseases as they traveled into new worlds, and Africa had some of the nastiest of all.

Yellow fever crossed the species divide from monkeys living in the canopies of west African forests into the indigenous human populations—who developed some resistance. Not so for Europeans. They would be bitten by mosquitoes, infected, and then die when their liver shut down and their insides turned to mush as the stomach and intestines began to bleed internally. The Spanish called this disease *vomito negro* ("black vomit"). Explorers carried the disease back to Europe and America, where it regularly cut deadly swathes through the population.

Dengue fever was an endemic African disease that caused extreme pain and suffering. It began with a sudden onset of fever followed by vomiting and a rash as well as migraine-like pains behind the ears and lower back pain. Severe cramping and muscular pain rotated around the body being particularly severe in the head, back, and limbs.

Microscopic parasites known as filariae caused immense pain and suffering. These tiny, worm-like animals penetrated a host's lymphatic system and prevented the body from draining impurities from the body. The tiny worms set up nests within the lymphatic system, preventing the drainage of fluids and causing elephantiasis with limbs swelling to a monstrous size, while the skin would become stiff and leather-like. Many explorers would return home, seemingly fit and healthy, only to develop debilitating symptoms years later.

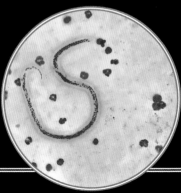

Microscopic worm: microfilaria

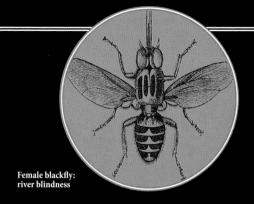

Female blackfly: river blindness

Even worse than this was the African disease of onchocerciasis—river blindness, which was spread by a tiny fly that lived near the fertile valleys of subtropical Africa. The filarial worm *Onchocerca volvulus* infested the area just beneath the skin, where the worms could be seen wriggling around. This caused unbearable itching: The discomfort was so intense that some people—desperate for relief—died due to suicide. The worms would lay up to 1,000 eggs a day and eventually migrated to the eyeballs, turning them milky white and blinding the sufferer.

A related and equally pernicious disease was African trypanosomiasis—sleeping sickness. This vicious disease was carried by the tsetse fly and from the get-go the symptoms were horrible. The large fly deposited worms under the skin into the host's subcutaneous tissue leaving swollen painful bites. Within three weeks the trypanosomes spread into the bloodstream and lymphatic system. Soon, the parasites began to eat away at the brain leading to spasms, blurred speech, confusion, and an irresistible urge to sleep.

By far the greatest scourge among explorers was malaria. Up to four species were endemic in Africa and while some strains were relatively benign others such as *P. falciparum* are absolutely deadly and can quickly kill even the healthiest victim. Colloquially known as "the shakes" or "the ague," malaria would periodically resurface—tormenting sufferers even if it did not kill them.

This vast range of diseases rendered much of central and tropical Africa as uninhabitable for Europeans. It is important to note that when Germany colonized Central West Africa and Papua New Guinea, they could only do so because no other power wanted to rule such a lethal biome. Another factor for explorers: Africa was the last continent to retain an assemblage of megafauna. Travelers faced constant danger from hungry lions, rampaging bull elephants, and spooked rhinos, in addition to a lethal array of biting reptiles and insects.

Tsetse fly: sleeping sickness

THE SOURCE OF THE NILE

For thousands of years the great mystery of the source of the Nile confounded many rulers. Egyptian pharaohs sent expeditions to find the source—as did Roman emperors. The Nile floods every year. The huge amounts of water that bring richness and life to the barren desert seemed to come from nowhere. Why was it so difficult to sail upstream and find the source?

We now know that the river's headwaters flow from Lake Victoria, but to reach this large body of water by simply sailing upriver is pretty much impossible. If sailing from Aswan to Khartoum, there are six sets of near-impassable and dangerous rapids. From Khartoum the river spreads out into a vast swampland interspersed with waterfalls that make it difficult to get to Lake Albert. Another waterfall protects Lake Victoria. And this is only the White Nile. James Bruce claimed he found the source of the Blue Nile, although this claim can be questioned. The vast distances involved, at 4,132 miles almost twice that of the 2,348 miles length of the Mississippi, and the dangers from hostile tribes, animals, and diseases made the journey all but impossible.

Richard Burton (1821–90) and John Hanning Speke (1827–64) solved this

LEFT AND BELOW While the Scotsman James Bruce claimed to have found the source of the Nile in the 1770s, this goal was only achieved almost a hundred years later.

Cairo · Suez
Nile R
EGYPT
Nile R · ARABIA
Nile R
Red Sea
Khartoum
AFRICA
Sudan · Lake Tana · Gulf of Aden
White Nile · Blue Nile
Lake Albert · Lake Kyoga
Kampala · Kenya
Lake Victoria
Ujiji · Tabora
Lake Tanganyika

Expedition Route
James Bruce 1769-73
Richard Burton and John Hanning Speke 1857-58

mystery by bypassing the Nile and heading straight to its headwaters from the east coast of Africa. It was still a daunting journey. On earlier expeditions the two explorers had heard of a large lozenge-shaped lake that could easily be the origin of the Nile. Setting out from Zanzibar (in modern Tanzania) in June 1857, the expedition, which included 130 men and thirty mules, headed for the Arab trading outpost of Tabora almost 600 miles from the coast. From there they planned to search for the mysterious lake.

John Hanning
Speke

Even before the expedition arrived at this midway point, both Burton and Speke were struck down by disease. Speke began raving as malarial fits coursed through his body, while Burton suffered from a creeping paralysis that incapacitated him for more than a year. Burton thought himself close to death; Speke's vision began to fade. But they recovered.

Upon finally reaching Tabora, the explorers heard that there were in fact two large lakes, Tanganyika and Victoria. In two canoes the party explored Lake Tanganyika, but could find no likely outlet. Speke then set out to the other lake and, naming it after Queen Victoria (reigned 1837–1901), proudly declared that he had found the source of the Nile. Burton, who had stayed behind to recuperate, was not convinced—but Speke's second expedition in 1860 proved that the main tributary of the Nile left from Lake Victoria.

This remarkable achievement did not apparently bring Speke any joy. He may have died by suicide in 1864, perhaps to escape the effects of debilitating illnesses picked up on his treks. However, some authorities report that the gunshot wound from which he died while shooting in Wiltshire, southern England, was accidental.

BELOW **Grant and Speke used local knowledge to help them find the true source of the Nile.**

David Livingstone

David Livingstone

David Livingstone was undoubtedly one of the greatest explorers the world has ever seen. He explored much of central and southern Africa: During his 29,000 miles of travel, he survived malaria, starvation, dysentery, and even an attack by a lion that saw his left arm reduced to shreds as the big cat crunched away—leaving more than ten puncture wounds in his flesh. He was the first European to cross the entire continent from west to east. During his expeditions some of the last great riddles of what lay at the center and in the south of Africa were answered.

After finishing his medical studies, Livingstone joined the London Missionary Society in 1838 and was soon ministering to sick Africans in the south of the continent. Filled with missionary zeal and determined to stamp out slavery, Livingstone set off on his first major expedition in 1849. In this remarkable journey, the explorer and his courageous wife Mary Moffat (1821-62) traveled north through the center of Africa. They crossed the Kalahari Desert and were the first Europeans to see Lake Ngami. There was a personal toll in this mammoth expedition. His two-month-old daughter died and so the remainder of his family were put on a fast boat back to England. Undaunted, Livingstone headed north again and came across the Zambesi River and the amazing Victoria Falls. He also progressed north to the Congo basin, before crossing Africa from Luanda on the Atlantic coast to Quelimane on the Indian Ocean coast in 1856.

BELOW Despite a dangerous run-in with a lion, David Livingstone managed to create an unsurpassed legacy of African exploration.

In 1858, Livingstone was back in Africa with Mary and several other relatives. Although he managed to record the mineral and agricultural resources of central and eastern Africa for the British government, and recorded Lake Chirous and Lake Nyasa—and also visited the Murchison Falls in what is now Uganda—it became a tragic trip when his wife died of fever in 1862.

ABOVE **Europeans and Africans were united in their grief when Livingstone eventually succumbed to a host of diseases and injuries.**

In 1866, Livingstone set off on his last expedition. Although Speke and Burton had found the source of the Nile, much more needed to be learned about the Nile, Congo, and Zambesi rivers. The explorer then disappeared. Several expeditions embarked in search of him. A relief party led by Welsh explorer Henry Morton Stanley (1841–1904) led the fifth mission to find him, and the famous meeting between the two men took place in 1871. When Stanley found Livingstone, in Ujiji near Lake Tanganyika in Tanzania, he reputedly uttered the famous line: "Dr. Livingstone, I presume?" Stanley found that the explorer was in ill health but still determined to find out why the Nile flooded each year.

Livingstone continued to explore the hostile central African environment. Of the sixty men who set out with him on his final expedition, only eleven survived. On May 1, 1873, Livingstone himself succumbed to a range of tropical diseases that had ravaged his gaunt body. When he was discovered in his hut, Livingstone was still kneeling in prayer. The explorer's heart was buried beneath a tree on the shores of Lake Tanganyika, while his preserved cadaver was taken to Zanzibar on the coast and then on to England where it was buried in Westminster Abbey, central London.

Missionaries, inspired by the explorer's experiences, flooded into Africa. His dramatic condemnation of the slave trade and its horrible practices—he wrote in his journals, "To overdraw its evils is an impossibility" and in a letter to the *New York Herald,* that if his comments led to the ending of the African East Coast slave trade, he would "regard that as a greater matter by far than the discovery of all the Nile sources together"—served to swing public opinion against the vile trade. Central Africa was opened up to further European exploration.

Mary Kingsley

Women made a tremendous contribution to the European exploration and settlement of Africa, but their achievements were largely overshadowed by the men that they accompanied. Not so English ethnographer Mary Kingsley (1862–1900). An intrepid woman, she was determined to explore African culture.

Kingsley was fascinated by the stories and memoirs penned by African explorers. Although not formally educated, she gained some schooling in tropical medicine. Then when her parents passed away in 1892, she used her inheritance to pursue her lifelong dream of traveling in Africa, asking the British Museum to help her find a natural history project that did not require a large capital outlay. The officials suggested that she collect specimens of beetles and fish. On the journey to Africa friendly sailors taught her the basics of navigation, a skill that would come in handy as she explored the wilds of Sierra Leone, Angola, and the Congo.

Mary Kingsley

As a single woman dressed in full Victorian regalia, Kingsley attracted a great deal of attention. When questioned why she did not wear more practical clothing than neck-to-ankle dresses, she is said to have replied: "You have no right to go about Africa in things you would be ashamed to be seen in at home." The respect Kingsley showed the natives was much at odds with the attitudes of many of her fellow explorers. She recognized that practices such as polygamy were useful for African circumstances—since she felt that in local conditions at the time there would be too much work for a single wife to manage—and did not condemn them out of hand as many of her fellow travelers did. She also criticized missionaries for their attempts to convert people from local religions. She did draw the line, however, at one of the cultural practices of the locals. It was believed that when twins were born, one of the offspring was devil's seed. Since it was impossible to tell which child was innocent and which child was evil, both were killed. The mother often suffered the same fate as she was blamed for attracting a devil.

Kingsley penetrated into many unexplored territories and faced many dangers. She developed a healthy respect for native animals and firmly believed in the importance of running away as soon as they were spotted. After her first trip, she returned with a solid reputation and such excellent specimens that the museum agreed to fund her next expedition.

In 1894, Kingsley returned to Africa and penetrated deep into the heart of Cameroon and Gabon, where she encountered the Fang people. She lived among them and her healing skills were much appreciated. They taught her how to survive in the wilderness and she was the first Westerner to canoe up the Ogowe River, where she collected specimens of fish previously unknown to Western science. Kingsley was also the first Westerner to climb Mount Cameroon, an active volcano 13,435ft high.

ABOVE AND RIGHT The wilds of Africa held
no fear for Mary Kingsley. Here she's shown
exploring the Ogowe River.

She was abandoned by her guides halfway up,
but continued on her own, only to find the peak
shrouded in mist, which blanketed the view.

Her most dangerous exploits came in
mid-1895 when she navigated the Rembwe
River. She fought off a leopard by hitting it on the
head with a cooking pot. She freed another
snared in a trap. At one stage her canoe was snagged while traversing a lagoon. A
swarm of crocodiles was beaten off with her paddle. Upon meeting some inhabitants
of a village in a jungle clearing she found a foul-smelling bag filled with the human
remains left over from a cannibal dinner.

While many Europeans died in the dreadful conditions of central Africa,
Kingsley's medical training helped her survive. One rule that she followed religiously
was to only drink water that had been boiled beforehand. Returning to England,
Kingsley wrote several best-selling books detailing her experiences and spoke to
many influential bodies. A theme that she returned to was the need to respect the
indigenous beliefs and practices of the African people.

On her last expedition, Kingsley became embroiled in the Second Boer War
(1899–1902) and died of typhoid on June 3, 1900, in Cape Town after nursing Boer
prisoners. Perhaps one of the most remarkable things about this extraordinary
woman is that no one has made a movie about her thrilling life.

Mary Kinglsey was not the only woman to make her mark in the world of
exploration in the Victorian era. Alexandrine Tinné (1835–69) from Holland
was the first European woman to attempt to cross the Sahara. Gertrude Bell (1868–
1926) made many expeditions to the Middle East and braved the harsh interior of the
Arabian Peninsula.

8 TO THE ENDS OF THE EARTH

ONCE IT WAS DETERMINED THAT THE WORLD WAS A GLOBE, one major challenge remained—getting to the north and the south poles. Explorers to these extreme regions of the globe faced a whole new set of difficulties. The average winter temperature in the Arctic is –30°F, and in Antarctica temperatures have reached as low as –128°F. Combined with fierce winds, deep crevices, shifting ice floes, and the ever-present danger of snow blindness, these temperatures meant that only the strongest could survive in these harsh environments. And even then, many of the toughest and most experienced explorers perished.

LEFT **Robert Falcon Scott looks at ease on the ice. But fatal misjudgements and mistakes doomed his party to an icy death.**

THE NORTHWEST PASSAGE

The search for the Northwest Passage was to Arctic exploration what the hunt for the fabled city of El Dorado was to the exploration of South America. Here the hope was that a sea route from the Atlantic Ocean through the dense Arctic Archipelago off the coast of Canada to the Pacific Ocean would lead to untold trading riches. Sadly for many explorers the dangers inherent in the attempt—not least the unpredictable, shifting ice floes that stretch for 900 miles from Canada's Baffin Island and over the Arctic Circle—would lead to frustration, failure, and even death.

Explorers could expect to be trapped in ice sheets for months at a time or blocked by towering 300ft glaciers. It took a canny and cunning Norwegian, Roald Amundsen (1872–1928), to finally unlock the icy route.

BELOW Traversing the Northwest Passage by boat seemed an impossible task. Amundsen, pictured in Antarctica, drew on all of his patience and experience to achieve the goal.

A History of Failure

The failed attempts to discover the Northwest Passage are almost too many to mention. John Cabot tried in 1497 and 1498 but could not pass. Jacques Cartier disappointed his king despite three attempts in the mid-sixteenth century. Spanish explorer Francisco de Ulloa set out in 1539 under the orders of Hernando Cortés but had no luck. Henry Hudson paid for the elusive search with his life in 1611. Even the redoubtable Captain James Cook, who mastered every ocean he sailed, was stymied in an attempt to find the elusive route. His sailing expertize was blocked by ice sheets that stretched over the horizon. With the advent of the Industrial Revolution, modern technology was thrown at the search for the Passage. Not always successfully.

Franklin's Expedition

One of the most tragic episodes in the quest to find the Northwest Passage was the 1845 expedition of British captain John Franklin (1786–1847). None of the 129 men who embarked with him would survive and they seemed to vanish from the face of the Earth. Only now is the mystery of the sad fate of this expedition being solved.

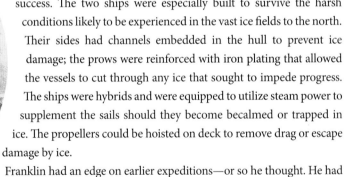

When his ships the HMS *Erebus* and HMS *Terror* left England in 1845 to search for a passage through the Arctic ice pack, its leader, Captain Franklin, had a firm expectation that his mission would be a roaring success. The two ships were especially built to survive the harsh conditions likely to be experienced in the vast ice fields to the north. Their sides had channels embedded in the hull to prevent ice damage; the prows were reinforced with iron plating that allowed the vessels to cut through any ice that sought to impede progress. The ships were hybrids and were equipped to utilize steam power to supplement the sails should they become becalmed or trapped in ice. The propellers could be hoisted on deck to remove drag or escape damage by ice.

John
Franklin

Franklin had an edge on earlier expeditions—or so he thought. He had laid in more than three years' supply of rations that used the latest technology: canned food. For the first time in the history of exploration, vitamin-rich food could be preserved for an indefinite period of time. Little did Franklin know as he set off on the journey that this infant technology would prove to be his undoing. The expedition ended in destruction, disease, and cannibalism. None of his crew members would live to tell the tale.

Franklin had something of a checkered history. Born in Spilsby, eastern England, with the scent of the North Sea in his nostrils, the young Franklin committed his life to service in the Royal Navy. He entered the service at the age of fourteen and saw his first taste of action at the Battle of Copenhagen (April 2, 1801) under Lord Nelson

(1758–1805). During the Napoleonic Wars, he steadily rose in rank while earning a reputation for bravery at the Battle of Trafalgar (October 21, 1805). Given his first command in 1818, Franklin headed straight to polar waters on a voyage of exploration to find the Northwest Passage. But halted by polar ice, he was forced to turn back. In 1819 he set off on a trek through the outer reaches of Canada. Franklin demonstrated his lack of flexibility on this journey and refused to turn back when the supplies began to run out. Things weren't helped when the commander apparently refused to let members of the officers class hunt for food or carry provisions and equipment. The thirty-six-month trek was a disaster. Eleven men died and, it is thought that the party had to resort to cannibalism.

Franklin's reputation was further sullied while serving in a posting in Van Diemen's Land. When the opportunity to lead an expedition to find the Northwest Passage arose in 1844, Franklin seized it in an effort to redeem his reputation.

The ships set off from Greenhithe, southeast England, on May 19, 1845. In July of that year the ships were seen in Baffin Bay by a whaling ship. The expedition then disappeared.

For several years nothing was heard of the *Erebus* and the *Terror*. In 1848, the first of many missions to find the missing mariners set out. Franklin had not planned a route beforehand, so the thirty-nine expeditions dispatched to find the explorers had a vast—not to mention hostile—area in which to search. Relying on accounts from local Inuit and tracking a possible route, the expeditions gradually pieced together the tragic fate of Franklin's expedition.

At first things went according to plan for Franklin and his crews. In 1845, ice in the Arctic was low and the ships made it past Baffin Bay near Greenland. They then continued north, threading their way between islands of the Canadian Arctic Archipelago. But just off King William Island the ocean froze and the vessels were stuck for the winter. This was to be expected, but when the weather stayed cold for the next two years the ships remained stuck. Franklin died on June 11, 1847, and was buried in a cairn on King William Island.

BELOW Franklin's expedition penetrated into the dangerous heart of the Canadian Arctic. None of his crew lived to tell the tale.

Twenty-four other members of the crew died and sometime in April 1848 the remaining crew abandoned the ships and began a hazardous 1,000-mile trek to the nearest trading post.

None of the crewmen made it even one-fifth of the way to safety. After following stories told by the Inuit, search parties found a trail of bones and abandoned equipment that stretched for hundreds of miles. In 1850, graves of some crewmen were found on Beechey Island, Canada. These men had died in the first year of the expedition, proving that something had gone seriously wrong even in the early stages of the journey.

The problem might have been those newfangled tin cans. The technology for the preservation of food was in its infancy and rather than soldering the can's lid on, workers had used lead as a sealant. It is thought that the metal contaminated the food, leading to extreme lead poisoning for the unsuspecting crew members. In 1981, the graves of three dead sailors were dug up on Beechey Island. These were the same graves that had been discovered in 1850. The three men—William Braine (1814–46), John Hartnell (c. 1821–46), and John Torrington (1825–46)—were perfectly preserved in the permafrost. Apart from slightly distended mouths and eyelids thanks to ice filling these cavities, the three looked almost as if they were still alive. During the autopsy, samples were taken from the three cadavers. Later tests revealed that all three had abnormally high levels of lead in their system. Torrington was emaciated thanks to prolonged poisoning and had high levels of lead in his system, which had aggravated a case of pneumonia.

BELOW **The crews of the trapped** *Terror* **and** *Erebus* **abandoned ship and embarked on an icy journey filled with cannibalism and starvation.**

Lead poisoning leads to several symptoms that may have contributed to the breakdown of the expedition. Sufferers' joints become inflamed and painful, they can't keep their food down, they feel fatigued and have headaches, suffer from memory loss, and their decision-making is impaired. Death follows in extreme cases of lead poisoning.

ABOVE **Although McClure traversed the Northwest Passage, not all of his crew survived. Here an explorer is buried in the ice.**

This might well account for the surviving crew members' decision to abandon ship. While not sure of the cause of their ills they must have known that the food supplies were tainted. Unable to eat the food and with scurvy making its presence felt, their only hope for survival was a desperate dash south. In another remarkable scientific find, bones of deceased expedition members have been recovered. Evidence of cut marks attest to cannibalism, which broke out as the crew members fought to survive the icy wastes. The remains were tested for DNA. The bones of some individuals were scattered over many miles. No doubt their corpses were carried by the fleeing crew and butchered and eaten as the hopeless journey progressed. Thirty-five bones recovered from Booth Point, now in Nunavut, and Erebus Bay on the west of Ross Island had been broken open and had signs of "pot polishing." This occurs when the ends of the boiling bones rub against the side of a pot as they are cooked. By cooking and breaking the bones the desperate crewmen, some who survived as late as 1850, could extract the last nutrients in marrow and soup stock from their shipmates' remains.

There is one remarkable twist to this epic tale of Arctic tragedy. In the years following the disaster, mariners reported an amazing sight. Icebergs were spotted floating in the Arctic with a large ship still locked in their icy grasp. Whether these reports were true is unknown, but in 2014–16 both the *Erebus* and the *Terror* were found resting on the ocean floor. One deepsea probe filmed one of the ship's galleys. Shelves well stocked, with canned food lining the cabin walls.

THE NORTHWEST PASSAGE SECURED

Franklin would have turned in his icy grave if he knew that a rescue effort sent to save his expedition resulted in the first successful crossing of the Northwest Passage. Many expeditions were sent to find the missing ships, but Commander Robert McClure (1807–73) was perhaps the most tenacious of all the explorers dispatched on this mission.

In a specially strengthened boat, the HMS *Investigator*—with large quantities of concentrates of lime and lemon to prevent scurvy—set out in January 1850. By July, McClure's ship had reached the Arctic Circle and penetrated deep into the ice floes, which were at a lower limit thanks to the warmth of the summer season. For the next month the ship cut its way through ice floes to reach open patches of water, but by September the ice closed in and the *Investigator* could not move any further. Undaunted, McClure loaded some of his men onto a sled and moved forward over the ice-covered frozen straits until there before him was Melville Island (part of the Canadian Arctic Archipelago) on the edge of the Arctic Ocean, which led to the Pacific. In front of the island was an ice-free body of water—now known as the McClure Strait. On October 31, 1850, he wrote in the ship's log that he had found the Northwest Passage.

For several more years, the ship was locked in the ice. A rescue by HMS *Resolute* found a message left by McClure. Using sleds, the crew of the *Resolute* traveled a short distance to find the survivors of the *Investigator*. McClure returned to Britain to a hero's welcome. Nevertheless, the Northwest Passage had still not been traversed by boat alone, but by a combination of sled and ship. Roald Amundsen would earn the honor of being the first to traverse the passage by boat—and go on to be the premier Arctic and Antarctic explorer.

LEFT The HMS *Investigator* was trapped in an ice floe on the north coast of Baring Island.

Roald Amundsen

Born in Borge, Norway, Roald Amundsen (1872–1928) proved himself a strong-willed individual from an early age. His parents were determined that he pursue a career in medicine; Amundsen disagreed, sold his medical textbooks and kit and set off for a life on the high seas. He served on sealers, gained a master's ticket, and in 1897 joined an expedition to the Antarctic aboard the Belgian-flagged *Belgica*. The expedition went awry and spent thirteen months trapped in ice. The young Norwegian assumed command and when the *Belgica* finally broke free in 1899, he became the first expedition leader to survive an Antarctic winter.

Inspired by his success, Amundsen decided to tackle the Northwest Passage. Whereas previous expeditions had taken the biggest ships possible, the Norwegian chose a small shallow-drafted sloop called the *Gjøa*, which only displaced 47 tons. With a compact crew of six, Amundsen set off in 1903. This expedition had one more crucial advantage: Rather than treating the Arctic as a foe to be overcome, Amundsen and his men sought to acclimatize to the harsh environment and make it their friend. When the *Gjøa* was locked in ice on King William Island the crew made friends with the indigenous Inuit and for two years learned their ways. The incomers adopted the local furs, which proved much more resistant to cold than woolen outfits. They learned hunting techniques and the art of driving dog teams and how to keep them alive in the harsh conditions. The crew even learned how to construct igloos and turn them into warm refuges from the icy winds.

BELOW **Amundsen used his huskies for transport and food. As the sleds became lighter, fewer dogs were required.**

Roald Amundsen

In August 1905, the ship was finally freed and resumed its westbound course. They scraped through many shallow waterways through the difficult reaches of the Canadian Arctic Archipelago. Three weeks later, in a brilliant moment of joy, the crew saw a whaler operating out of San Francisco on the Pacific. Even though the tiny boat was locked in ice again, Amundsen knew that in the following thaw he would be able to carry on the journey through the Bering Strait and succeed in his mission.

The plucky Norwegian was determined to tell the world of his achievements and did not want to wait for the thaw. Demonstrating his impressive abilities, he set off with a crewman across the frozen wastes to Eagle City in Alaska, where he knew there was a telegraph office. This journey was quite remarkable. With one sled and one dog team, they had to traverse 500 miles of snow and ice and scale mountains almost 9,000ft high. On December 5, 1905, the two men reached Eagle City and the amazing accomplishments were telegraphed to the world. A short journey through the Bering Strait and the Northwest Passage had finally been traversed. It was not until 1942 that the passage was crossed again by Henry Larsen (1899–1964) of the Canadian Mounted Police. Now, of course, with climate change, the Northwest Passage is less trecherous. In 2007, for the first time in recorded history, the entire passage was ice-free.

BELOW **Amundsen plants the Norwegian flag at the South Pole. This flag would break Falcon Scott's heart and spirit.**

THE SOUTH POLE

Amundsen had one major rival in the race to the South Pole: British explorer Captain Robert Falcon Scott (1868–1912). One man would triumph, while the other would perish in the wastes of Antarctica.

Robert Falcon Scott

Amundsen's expedition ran like clockwork. Proceeding from the Madeira Islands, he sailed his ship the *Fram* directly to the Bay of Whales and into the Ross Sea. He had planned for the trip in a meticulous fashion and even had food stores dumped along his possible route. To transport his supplies, Amundsen's party used fifty-two dogs and four sleds loaded with food, tents, and paraffin to keep them warm. In a brilliantly unsentimental feat of planning, the expedition not only used the dogs as transport but also ate them when supplies ran out and the sleds became lighter.

Leaving from the closest possible location to the South Pole, Amundsen set out on October 19, 1911. Good weather blessed the expedition and on December 14, the explorers were the first humans to reach the South Pole. Here they erected the Norwegian flag, a symbol of their accomplishment.

TOP Scott took this photo of his expedition's pony-drawn sleds. The horses could not survive and Scott and his men had to tow the heavy loads.

This very flag would break the hearts of Captain Scott and his companions when they reached the same location barely a month later. In a striking photo taken on January 17, 1912, Scott and his four men posed in front of the Norwegian flag, the dreadful disappointment they felt at not being the first to the South Pole evident on their faces.

Although Scott arrived in Antarctica at the same time as his Norwegian rival, he took a longer route from McMurdo Sound. Bad weather and rough terrain compounded his problems and he and his four companions found the going exceedingly difficult. Adding to the dire situation was his decision to use Siberian ponies and motorized sleds, none of which could function in the Antarctic chill, so Scott and his four companions had to pull supply sleds themselves.

Perhaps when the fateful photo was taken, the men already knew that they were doomed. Supplies were low and when they turned to begin their journey back to the coastal depot it had to be done on foot. The woolen clothes that Scott had chosen allowed the chill to settle in. With frostbite in their limbs, malnourished and most likely suffering from scurvy, they set off home.

One crew member, Edgar Evans (1876–1912), fell in the ice and died from a head wound. Lawrence Oates (1880–1912), failing and weak, left the frozen tent one night saying he might be gone for "some time," sacrificing himself so the others would not be slowed down. By the end of March Scott and his last two companions died in a blizzard only 12 miles from their depot and safety. Their bodies and the flimsy tent that they died in were not discovered for several years. Scott lay frozen between the corpses of Henry "Birdie" Bowers (1883–1912) and Edward Wilson (1872–1912).

Even though the South Pole had been reached, the Antarctic was by no means conquered. British explorer Ernest Shackleton (1874–1922) set off with twenty-seven men in the *Endurance* in December 1914 with the goal of being the first man to cross the frozen continent. They did not even reach the Antarctic landmass. While trying to batter through ice floes on the Weddell Sea, the ship was trapped by pack ice and, on November 21, 1915, was crushed and sank beneath the sea. For several months the shipwrecked crew survived on the open ice, eating seals, penguins, and their dogs. In April, with the spring melt, the crew set off in salvaged lifeboats, encountering killer whales and storms before they managed to land on Elephant Island. Shackleton took his five strongest men and set off again to South Georgia Island in a desperate last effort to find succor. After an 800-mile journey, they found help, and returning to Elephant Island found that the rest of the crew had survived.

BELOW Scott's expedition found Amundsen's tent and a note therein. They would be dead within two months.

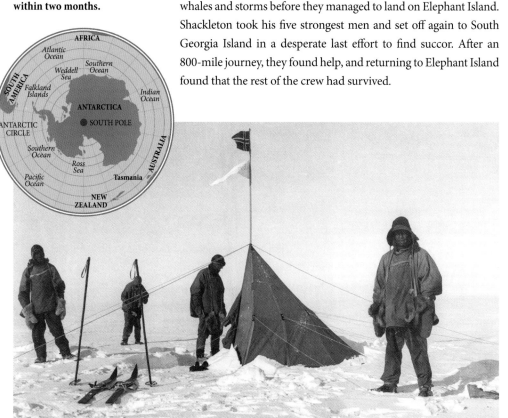

Preserved for Posterity: Shackleton's and Mawson's Huts

Two remarkable artifacts remain from the exploration of Antarctica. They are not a collection of boots or a couple of books, but intact huts of two major expeditions filled with all of the paraphernalia and everyday items used by these early explorers.

Shackleton's hut at Cape Royds on Ross Island—erected during an earlier attempt to be first to the South Pole, during his *Nimrod* expedition in 1908—is quite large, because fifteen explorers had to be accommodated. It is still exactly as it was left when the men departed. A stove still sports a kettle, a cooking pot, and even a skillet complete with a half-cooked pancake! Tins of food and medicine bottles line the shelves, while a table pushed up against a wall is covered in mitts and shoes. Outside of the hut are the remnants of a stable built for Siberian ponies and a garage for the first ever automobile used in Antarctica (a 15hp Arrol-Johnston). A remarkable find was made in 2010: The original explorers left in such a hurry that they left behind five crates of whiskey and brandy. The hoard was dug up and returned to New Zealand for "scientific experiments."

Sir Douglas Mawson (1882–1958) accompanied Shackleton on some of his ill-fated expeditions, but went on to

ABOVE **Mawson's Hut at Cape Denison is a valuable time capsule that shows the primitive conditions explorers of Antarctica had to endure.**

make a name for himself as Australia's greatest Antarctic explorer. Mawson's hut, built during the explorer's Australasian Antarctic Expedition of 1911–14, is located at Cape Denison in Commonwealth Bay. It was filled with ice and snow until an Australian restoration project removed 1,200 cubic ft of ice and restored the roof. It is a smaller structure than Shackleton's hut but still includes a kitchen, sleeping quarters, and a storeroom. There are many fascinating artifacts within the hut, including primitive generators, framed photographs, and books on the shelves that line the wall. A bowl of desiccated peas still lies on the kitchen bench—no doubt waiting for the pot!

Robert E. Peary

THE NORTH POLE

Two men competed with each other to be the first to conquer the North Pole. Unlike Captain Scott, they both survived with their lives, but their reputations were tarnished.

Robert E. Peary (1856–1920) demonstrated many characteristics that would currently be seen as typical of someone suffering from narcissistic personality disorder. From an early age he declared that he was above the common ruck of fellow men and would be known one day for a remarkable achievement. He was an abrasive fellow who alienated many of his companions, including his rival in the race to the North Pole, American explorer Frederick Cook (1865–1940), and he oscillated between wild optimism and crashing despair. Nevertheless, Peary was determined. In one expedition his boots were pulled off and eight frostbitten toes came off with them! Undaunted, the explorer taught himself to walk again without a trace of a limp.

Trained as a marine engineer, Peary was fascinated by the vast icefields of Greenland. In 1886, he was part of an expedition into the interior of this frozen country and at one stage the ship on which he was traveling was trapped in the Inglefield Gulf on the northwest coast. He and his companion were forced to cross the top end of the country to find succor and to return to his ship—in doing so, the pair proved that Greenland was an island.

BELOW **Robert Peary and his team erected this ice tower at the North Pole in April 1909.**

RIGHT **A member of Cook's expedition shows the essentials of Arctic exploration: snow shoes, skis, and a water-proof tent.**

Peary then turned his attention to the Canadian Arctic. Here he learned the ways of the Inuit and began to realize that, using their specialized knowledge, he could reach the North Pole. The American government became interested in the expedition and funded Peary, enabling him to purchase the SS *Roosevelt*, a 1,600-ton cutter fitted out for Arctic conditions. In July 1908, Peary set out. Collecting some Inuit on the way, the party wintered at Cape Columbia and on March 1, 1909, set off for the pole. After a trek of 400 miles, they finally reached the North Pole on April 6, 1909.

Or so he said. Although Peary was welcomed back to the United States as a hero and retired as a rear admiral, there are some who maintain he never actually reached his destination. Some of his charts are inaccurate, his diary was remarkably clean given the journey it had been on, and the writing was remarkably neat for a man wearing mittens. Key pages were blank.

Frederick Cook, a onetime comrade of Peary, claimed to have reached the North Pole on April 21, 1908, but for some reason did not announce his accomplishment until September 1909. Cook's claim came in for some close questioning. After the journey his sled was still in an almost pristine condition and the party made suspiciously rapid progress despite the rough terrain. One of the Inuit companions stated that they had only traveled a few miles from land.

In the ensuing controversy Peary won the battle of public opinion and was confirmed as the first to reach the North Pole, while Cook was jailed for corporate fraud. New photogrammetric examination of the pictures taken at what Peary claimed was the pole tends to confirm his claim.

Even though Peary probably reached the North Pole and seemingly beat Roald Amundsen to this goal, the Norwegian still had one trick up his sleeve. With an Italian-crewed Zeppelin airship named *Norge* he became the first person to fly over the North Pole on May 12, 1926.

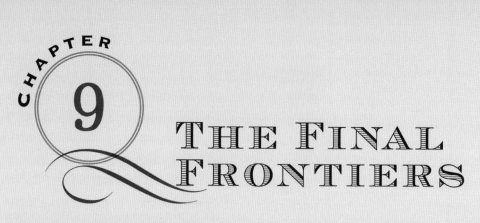

CHAPTER 9

THE FINAL FRONTIERS

IN THE TWENTIETH CENTURY, people and their machines soared through the stratosphere and beyond, escaping the pull of Earth's gravity. The same gravitational forces have restricted the depth at which humans have been able to penetrate below the surface of the ocean.

Pioneers such as Auguste Piccard (1884–1962) unshackled human potential by exploring both the stratosphere in a balloon, and the deep ocean in his pressurized "bathyscaphe." The free-diving, self-propelled submersible reached a depth of 10,335ft in 1953, proving that humans could live in the highly pressurized deep-sea environment.

LEFT Piccard managed to reach the stratosphere in this remarkable contraption. A life-support gondola was strung below a huge balloon.

THE SPACE RACE

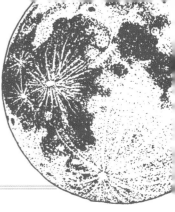

In a landmark speech on September 12, 1962, U.S. President John F. Kennedy (1917–63) announced plans to put humans on the moon. He spoke of an optimistic future for exploring beyond our atmosphere:

"WE HAVE VOWED THAT WE SHALL NOT SEE SPACE FILLED WITH WEAPONS OF MASS DESTRUCTION, BUT WITH INSTRUMENTS OF KNOWLEDGE AND UNDERSTANDING ... FOR SPACE SCIENCE, LIKE NUCLEAR SCIENCE AND ALL TECHNOLOGY, HAS NO CONSCIENCE OF ITS OWN. WHETHER IT WILL BECOME A FORCE FOR GOOD OR ILL DEPENDS ON MAN."

These words have proved to be prescient. While space exploration has demonstrated the best that humans can do when cooperating internationally, it has recently become something altogether more threatening. Could space exploration be replaced by a space arms race?

In his famous speech Kennedy threw down the gauntlet to the Soviet Union when he invited the Americans and their allies to put a human being on the moon before 1970. This was a vast undertaking as so many of the technologies needed by astronauts existed in theory only. No suitable space suits had been designed, the means of eliminating waste was a mystery, and there was no method of adapting food and water for use in zero gravity.

BELOW **President Kennedy makes his moon-landing announcement.**

Kennedy took the risk. His words were inspiring:

"But if I were to say, my fellow citizens, that we shall send to the moon, 240,000 miles away from the control station in Houston, a giant rocket more than 300ft tall, the length of this football field, made of new metal alloys, some of which have not yet been invented, capable of standing heat and stresses several more than have ever been experienced, fitted together with a precision better than the finest watch, carrying all the equipment needed for propulsion, guidance, control, communications, food, and survival, on an untried mission to an unknown celestial body, and then return it safely to Earth, re-entering the atmosphere at speeds over 25,000 miles per hour, causing heat about half that of the temperature of the sun ... and do all this, and do it right, and do it first before this decade is out—then we must be bold."

Remarkably, even though the president did not live to see it, his vision was realized. On July 20, 1969, *Apollo 11* landed on the moon. But for all of JFK's idealistic words, his key motivation was to make darn sure that the United States would win the space race against its Cold War enemies, the communist Soviet Union.

Americans first knew they were on the back foot in October 1957 when the Russians launched their first *Sputnik 1* ("Co-traveler 1"). The strange, beach-ball-sized device was the first man-made device put into orbit. It emitted a simple repetitive electronic single with no other meaning than to declare "I am here."

In the context of the Cold War (1947–91) between the capitalist West and the communist East, this was a momentous shift in the balance of power. It clearly signaled that the Soviet Union would be able to send nuclear weapons anywhere on the globe. Americans were terrified. It also threw down a moral gauntlet—Americans, with their can-do sense of optimism, were being beaten by a totalitarian state.

BELOW **Sputnik 1 was the first man-made object put into orbit. The simple Soviet device thrilled, and terrified, the American public.**

RIGHT Laika was the first living creature to orbit the Earth. The mutt made history but did not live to enjoy it.

Sputnik 2 was launched soon after, in November 1957. This was designed as an experiment to determine if living creatures could survive being sent into space. A stray mongrel terrier called Laika ("Barker") was taken from the streets of Moscow and launched beyond the atmosphere to become the first creature (apart from microbes) to enter Earth's orbit.

The 13lb terrier was placed within a pressurized and padded cabin with enough room for her to stand or lie down. Sustenance was dispensed in a gelatinized form and electrodes were strapped to her body to beam vital signs back to Earth. These did not last for long. The craft rapidly overheated and the dog died of heat stress after four orbits over several hours. The Soviets hid this fact and claimed that the little dog lived for almost a week.

American anxiety continued to grow. Several botched attempts to launch a satellite made things even worse. Fortunately, a solution was at hand. For several years the German scientist Wernher von Braun (1912–77) had been building the *Juno* multistage rocket-launching system. Named after a Greek goddess, the rocket was designed to carry payloads into orbit as simply as possible. After a successful

launch on January 31, 1958, *Explorer 1*, the first American satellite, entered Earth's orbit. The multistage rocket systems designed by Braun and his team laid the foundation for the successful rocket launches of the following decades. That same year, U.S. President Dwight D. Eisenhower (1890–1969) established the National Aeronautics and Space Administration (NASA) to take the fight up to the Soviets.

LEFT Wernher von Braun (at right) holds up a model of the future of American space exploration. Early rockets would evolve into *Saturn V*.

Nazis in Space

In the closing years of World War II, Nazi leader Adolf Hitler (1889–1945) directed huge amounts of funding at the German rocket program run by von Braun. At the Peenemünde rocket-testing range, the talented aerospace engineer Wernher von Braun developed the ballistic V-2 rocket. He always thought that humanity's destiny lay in space and he was able to conveniently forget that his rockets were built with slave labor and were to be armed with payloads of high explosives and dropped on civilian targets.

Nevertheless, Braun did make huge strides in the science of launching stabilized aerodynamic rockets into space.

LEFT **After the war, hundreds of disassembled V-2s were taken to the U.S. aboard Liberty Ships. These were reassembled and formed the basis of the American space program.**

ABOVE **Von Braun and many other Nazi scientists had their records altered in "Operation Paperclip" to allow them to make their way to America.**

When the war ended both the Soviets and the Americans made tremendous efforts to secure Nazi technology and weapons for their own research purposes. The Americans hit the jackpot when they enlisted von Braun with his team of scientists, all on the cutting edge of their fields of research.

During the space race von Braun was the ace in the United States' hands and his development of the multistage Saturn series of rockets gave NASA a reliable means of reaching space.

Another German scientist who was smuggled into America was Hubertus Strughold. Many of the results of his fatal experiments carried out in Dachau Concentration Camp were used to develop life support systems in the Saturn program.

Pressure continued to mount. In 1959, the Soviets launched *Luna 2*—a space probe that hit the moon. On April 12, 1961, three months after President Kennedy's inauguration, Soviet cosmonaut Yuri Gagarin (1934–68) became the first human to orbit the moon and return safely, aboard the satellite *Vostok 1*.

At 9 a.m. Moscow time on that day, the rocket was launched. It circled the planet at a distance of between 109 miles and 203 miles. The trip lasted for 108 minutes and while in orbit Gagarin was able to observe the Earth through three portholes while monitoring the on-board systems and dictating his observations.

The Soviets had obviously picked the right man for the job. During the launch—when Gagarin's pilot seat ejected at a height of more than 4 miles, and when his parachute deployed at around 8,000ft above the Earth—his blood pressure and pulse stayed constant.

Earth

Yuri Gagarin was made a hero of the Soviet Union. But his luck did not last. On March 27, 1968, this brave explorer would be killed in a failed test flight.

By 1962, NASA's lunar landing program was finally in place. Project *Apollo* was granted huge sums of money. NASA grew into a massive enterprise, employing tens of thousands of scientists and production staff.

In the years leading up to 1969, the *Apollo* program made great strides in exploring the solar system. On December 24, 1968, *Apollo 8* made the first successful orbit of the moon by a manned vessel. *Apollo 9* and *Apollo 10* laid the groundwork for the next mission, which would actually land on the moon—*Apollo 11*.

LEFT AND BELOW **Gagarin was the first to carry out the traditional Soviet cosmonaut practice of urinating on the wheel of the bus taking him to his spaceship!**

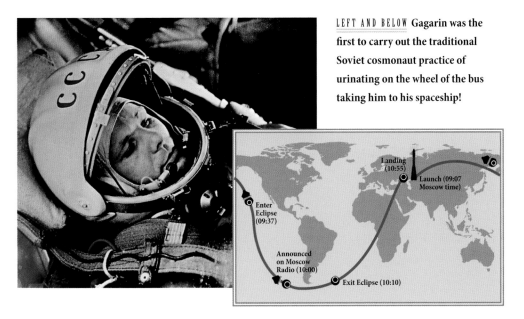

Landing (10:55)

Launch (09:07 Moscow time)

Enter Eclipse (09:37)

Announced on Moscow Radio (10:00)

Exit Eclipse (10:10)

First Woman in Space

Valentina Vladimirovna Tereshkova (born 1937) reached space at the age of only twenty-six when she orbited the Earth forty-eight times as a crewmember of *Vostok 6* in June 1963. The mission was intended to only last for twenty-four hours, but she toughed it out for three whole days even though she could not leave her seat. This expedition broke new ground and placed the Soviet Union firmly in the lead in the space race. The Russians had a few more tricks up their sleeves in the propaganda war. She easily beat the orbits made by the previous six American *Mercury* capsules and while orbiting she beamed down a live TV broadcast to the Soviet media.

The Russians actually had two capsules orbiting the Earth at the time, and Valentina was in frequent radio contact with her compatriot Valery Bykovsky (1934–2019), who was manning *Vostok 5*. The two vessels came within 3 miles of one another at one point and they both landed back on Earth on June 19, 1963. Beginning in 1961, the Russians trained six female cosmonauts who had to pass the same rigorous training as the men.

BELOW **Valentina Vladimirovna Tereshkova was selected from a pool of elite female cosmonauts to be the first woman in space.**

Even though the mission to land men on the moon might seem worlds away from the historical seaborne exploration of the Pacific and Atlantic oceans, it was in many ways similar. All of the early explorers would sail their ship toward a new land and a small party in a row boat would go inshore to scout out the terrain before returning to the "mother" ship to report their findings. A similar process was used on *Apollo 11*.

On July 16, 1969, three astronauts— Neil Armstrong (1930–2012), Edwin "Buzz" Aldrin (born 1930), and Michael Collins (born 1930)—were blasted from Cape Kennedy in Florida on the tip of a 364ft-high, 155-million horsepower *Saturn V* rocket in the *Apollo 11* command capsule. On July 19, the spaceship entered the moon's orbit and separated from the third stage of the *Saturn V* rocket. The next day, Armstrong and Aldrin climbed through the narrow hatch out of the command module into *Eagle*—the moon lander. The two craft separated and the lander descended toward the surface of the moon, while Collins, manning the command capsule *Columbia*, continued in orbit.

FAR LEFT AND ABOVE **Armstrong, Collins, and Aldrin successfully reached the moon. A jealous Soviet Union started the rumor that the mission was a hoax.**

This was a very hazardous stage of the exploration. The command capsule and its rescue rocket circled behind the moon several times and lost contact with Armstrong and Aldrin. Should something have gone wrong, Collins would not have been able to assist.

Nothing did go wrong and at 8.17 p.m. UTC (Coordinated Universal Time), *Eagle* set down on the surface of the moon. Initial plans had stipulated a six-hour rest period for the crew, but human nature being what it is, curiosity and a love of exploration drove the men out. At 2:56 a.m. UTC, on July 21, Neil Armstrong became the first man to walk on the surface of a celestial body. The Americans had won the space race.

Allies such as Australia made a valuable contribution to the mission by relaying vital data and signals from the lunar module. Even the Russians monitored American radio traffic from a facility in the southern part of the Soviet Union. Unable to compete, they gave up their intentions to land on the moon and admitted that the West had won.

"THAT'S ONE SMALL STEP FOR MAN, ONE GIANT LEAP FOR MANKIND."

—NEIL ARMSTRONG

The three astronauts were allowed little rest after the splashdown in the Pacific Ocean. Soon after they were debriefed, the trio set off on a journey that rivaled the great voyages of the past. In forty-five days they visited twenty-four countries as they flew around the world on *Air Force II*. Britain's Queen Elizabeth II, Pope John Paul I, and the king of Thailand were among the estimated 100 million people who turned out to greet the explorers as part of the "Giant Leap" world tour. Needless to say, the Soviet Union was not on the itinerary.

Space exploration after *Apollo 11* became less partisan. With less cash to spend and more pressing issues on the agenda, the great powers put space travel on the back-burner. Cooperation rather than competition became the watchword, and in 1975 an *Apollo* mission delivered three American astronauts to a Soviet-made *Soyuz* orbiter, where a symbolic handshake in space set the scene for international cooperation in space exploration that continues to this day with the International Space Station, launched in 1998.

ABOVE **The International Space Station represents humanity's first permanent presence in space. In 1975, astronauts and cosmonauts shook hands in a symbol of goodwill.**

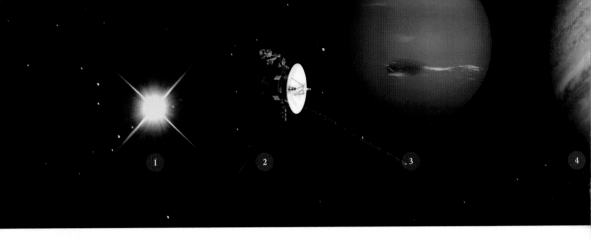

AGE OF THE SPACE PROBE

The last five decades have seen a new type of explorer—the space probe. Equipped to fly farther and faster than manned ships, space probes and their cousins, the surface landers, are vital for humanity's exploration of our solar system and deep space beyond.

Viking

On July 20, 1976, humans saw the surface of Mars close up for the first time. An image from *Viking 1*, which had just landed on the planet, showed a dusty soil interspersed with jagged rocks and stones. A picture taken soon afterward showed the horizon stretching off into the distance. Other pictures of geological formations proved that water had once coursed over the surface of the "Red Planet." Deep valleys, river courses, and even ancient ocean beds attested to long-vanished seas fed by storm clouds and rain. As well as taking photos of their surroundings, the landers deployed sensors designed to carry out chemical analysis and search for signs of life. No definitive answer was found to the question of whether there was life on Mars.

Voyagers 1 and *2*

Both *Voyagers* were launched by NASA in 1977. *Voyager 1* was aimed at Jupiter, Saturn, and Titan—Saturn's largest moon—passing by rather than landing. The probe studied the rings surrounding the two planets and measured their weather patterns and magnetic fields while taking detailed photos of the planets' surfaces. In 1980, *Voyager 1* reached escape velocity to leave the gravitational pull of the sun and drove itself out of the solar system. In 2012, it escaped the heliopause (the limits of solar winds) and entered intergalactic space. Remarkably, the probe still communicates with NASA and, despite being the furthest human-made object from Earth—13.6 billion miles away at the time of writing—it still accepts commands from mission control.

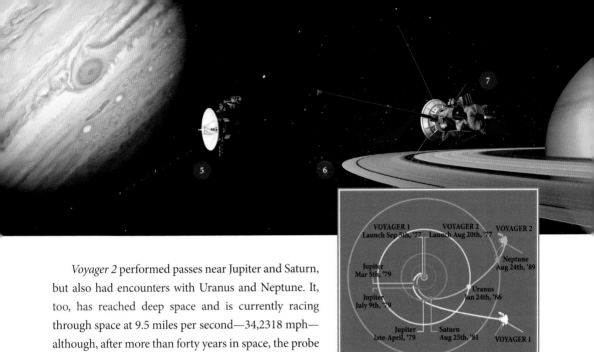

Voyager 2 performed passes near Jupiter and Saturn, but also had encounters with Uranus and Neptune. It, too, has reached deep space and is currently racing through space at 9.5 miles per second—34,2318 mph—although, after more than forty years in space, the probe is still only 16 light hours from Earth. In 296,000 years or so, Voyager 2 should pass 4.3 light years from Sirius—the famous "Dog Star"—which is 8.6 light years distant from Earth.

Both probes are expected to keep transmitting until 2025.

ABOVE The two Voyager probes were sent into space in 1977 and followed the same trajectory until they parted ways after passing Jupiter.

Cassini

Formally known as the Cassini-Huygens space research mission, this remarkable journey of exploration combined a probe and a lander. The successful mission, launched in 1997, gave NASA, the European Space Agency, and the Italian Space Agency a tremendous understanding of Saturn, its rings, and the moons surrounding the planet. In 2004, Cassini became the first craft to enter the planetary giant's orbit and spent thirteen years photographing Saturn's rings and the gaseous surface before it was de-orbited and plunged into the outer atmosphere in 2017. In this final mission, it sent back vital readings regarding the chemical makeup of Saturn's atmosphere.

Meanwhile, the Huygens lander successfully reached the surface of Saturn's largest moon, Titan, on January 14, 2005. This was the first landing on a celestial body in the outer solar system, and remarkable photos of an icy surface and a methane-rich atmosphere were sent back to Earth.

In February 2019, the Japanese probe Hayabusa2 (Japanese for "Peregrine Falcon") performed the stunning feat of landing on an asteroid that was traveling at speed around the sun while spinning like a top. The probe had to approach the small asteroid 162173 Ryugu and find a place to land on its rocky surface, which only has a diameter of around 3,000 ft.

To the Bottom of the Ocean Deep

IT MAY BE SAID THAT exploration of the ocean deep began with Ferdinand Magellan, who sought to plumb the depths of the Pacific Ocean in the fifteenth century. He attached an iron ball to 2,300ft of rope and sent it deep into the ocean, but it never hit the ocean floor.

The true depth of the ocean was only determined in the twentieth century, with the use of sophisticated sonar and radar technology. The deepest feature is the Marianas Trench in the Pacific Ocean. This vast, crescent-shaped trench is 6.8 miles at its deepest. If Mount Everest was placed in this trench its top would still be more than a mile underwater!

Of course the pressure at such a depth is immense (8 tons per square inch), but one man penetrated to the bottom of Challenger Deep (the deepest marine trench in the world) using a remarkable device that was similar to Magellan's earliest depth finder—an object that used gravity to reach the bottom.

The acclaimed Canadian movie director James Cameron (born 1954) poured much of his wealth into the creation of the solo deep-sea craft *Deepsea Challenger* so that he could explore Challenger Deep.

ABOVE **James Cameron sank many millions of dollars into deepsea exploration.**

This three-story-high submarine was designed to sink like an iron cannonball as quickly as possible at 500ft per minute.

This ensured that Cameron, one of the few men to reach the bottom of the Marianas Trench, only took two and a half hours to sink to his destination. He then had more time to use the sub's scientific instruments, "claws," and "slurper" to gather data and film superb 3D images.

This fascinating expedition from March 2012 showed that humans can learn more when exploring the "hadal zone" below 20,000ft depth. Some farsighted scientists see the *Deepsea Challenger* as the perfect device for humans to use if we ever get the chance to explore the watery moon Europa.

THE FUTURE OF SPACE EXPLORATION

The *Europa Clipper* and *Europa Lander* missions are still on the drawing board, but they are fantastically exciting. Previous flybys of Jupiter's moon Europa have shown that it is a celestial body completely covered in water, with an icy crust 10–15 miles thick. This crust is constantly moving and shifting, just like our own planet's tectonic plates, demonstrating the existence of a living core that sends up hydrothermal gases at the bottom of Europa's ocean.

There may be diverse species of water-dwelling animals and plants, rivaling those found on Earth—maybe even intelligent life? The *Clipper*, intended to be launched in the third decade of this century, will scout suitable locations for a lander to set down on the surface of this fascinating moon and then look for biological signatures.

Maybe this expedition will finally prove that "we are not alone." At the time of writing, certain high-flying tech wizards are talking about uploading human consciousness onto an electronic host— maybe "humans" will reach the stars soon!

BELOW This is an artist's impression of what a lander on Europa may look like. It will be equipped with sensors designed to detect signs of life.

Space Monkeys

The Soviet dog Laika was not the only critter to be sent into space. Apes and monkeys are considered to be perfect subjects for experiments that test the effects of space travel on people since they are so closely related to us. Many different types of primates have been shot into space. They are usually sedated to keep them calm on what would otherwise be terrifying trips.

The United States' first jet-propelled primate was Albert the Rhesus Macaque, who was strapped into a V-2 rocket in 1948. Quite a few "Alberts" were sent into space including Albert III, who was a crab-eating macaque. Squirrel monkeys were also used by the Americans, as were some pig-tailed macaques.

Argentina sent a tufted capuchin named Juan aloft in 1969, and in 2001 China sent a rabbit, a monkey, and a dog into space aboard a *Shenzhou II* rocket.

BELOW **Ham the chimp was launched into suborbital space in 1961. During the trip he pulled some levers when prompted by lights and survived to tell the tale!**

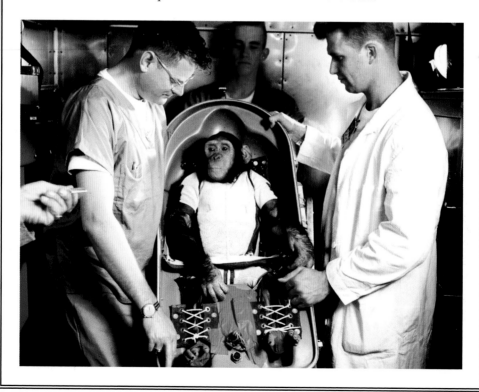

DESTINATION MARS

Recent missions have proved that Mars was once a watery world. The two Mars rovers, *Spirit* and *Opportunity*, found pebbles that had been rounded by thousands of years of running water. Almost 2 percent of the "soil" of Mars has been revealed to be water. The Martian north pole used to be covered by a huge body of water covering one-fifth of the planet—no doubt there are still large amounts of frozen water at the poles, just awaiting discovery and exploitation.

NASA's *Mars Reconnaissance* orbiter, launched in 2005, has photographed 99 percent of the planet's surface in the course of 60,000 orbits. Detailed photos have revealed clues for how humans can colonize the "Red Planet." In some locations meltwater or ice avalanches have been detected on the surface during the Mars summer, and remnants of a deep-sea hydrothermal vent system have been found. Just as on Earth, these locations are a hotspot in which a vast range of useful minerals can be found.

Should a colony be founded, any explorers will be the first independent interplanetary explorers. The distances are vast. When the Earth and Mars planets are at their furthest apart, around 250 million miles separate them. At the closest, which only occurs once every two years, they are approximately 34 million miles apart. A radio signal can take up to twenty minutes to pass between the two planets.

Given these difficulties, any human explorers who reach the "Red Planet" will have to be self-sufficient from the outset. They will have to make their own fuel, grow their own food, and replenish their oxygen supplies from water found on the planet. 3D printers will probably be used to make housing and equipment. New technologies will allow the settlers to use electrolysis to split water

Mars

BELOW **The differing orbits of Mars and Earth limits the opportunities for human expeditions to the Red Planet.**

Mars rover, *Opportunity*

into its constituent atoms, producing hydrogen rocket fuel and oxygen. Fortunately, the Martian crust could potentially have vast deposits of iron, gold, nickel, and other vital resources for human settlement.

Where will the know-how for such technology come from? In all likelihood, humanity will have to put permanent colonies of explorers on the moon to "road test" the new kit. India has made a vital contribution toward this goal. In 2008, the lunar orbiter *Chandrayaan 1* confirmed the presence of subterranean ice deposits on the moon's polar caps and these will most likely be the location of future exploration and settlement. Even now, NASA and some private-enterprise partners are planning a permanent presence. An orbiting spaceship called *Gateway* will orbit the moon and provide support for human and robotic missions. The Russians intend to have boots on the moon by 2030, and other powers including China are looking at similar options. Any craft launched from the moon will require a fraction of the fuel needed to launch a rocket out of Earth's atmosphere.

BELOW **New planets are being discovered all of the time. Many are in the "goldilocks zone"—not too hot, not too cold—just right.**

Just as the Portuguese, Spanish, and the Vikings leapfrogged from established islands on their way to the New World, so humanity may find its way to Mars. Hopefully exploration of Mars and beyond will be science fact—not science fiction.